The Cold War

A History in Documents

"All the News That's Fit to Print"

The New York Times

CITY EDITION

Weather: Showers, warm today; clear tonight. Sunny, pleasant tomorrow. Temp. range: today 81-66; Sunday 77-66. Temp.-Hum. Index yesterday 69. U.S. report on P. 50.

VOL. CXVIII....No. 40,721 — NEW YORK, MONDAY, JULY 21, 1969 — 10 CENTS

MAN WALKS ON MOON

ASTRONAUTS LAND ON A PLAIN AFTER STEERING PAST CRATER

Voice From Moon: 'Eagle Has Landed'

EAGLE (the lunar module): Houston. Tranquility Base here. The Eagle has landed.

HOUSTON: Eagle, we copy you on the ground. You've got a bunch of guys about to turn blue. We're breathing again. Thanks a lot.

TRANQUILITY BASE: Thank you.

HOUSTON: You're looking good here.

TRANQUILITY BASE: A very smooth touchdown.

HOUSTON: Eagle, you are stay for T1. [The first step in the lunar operation.] Over.

TRANQUILITY BASE: Roger. Stay for T1.

HOUSTON: Roger and we see you venting the ox.

TRANQUILITY BASE: Roger.

COLUMBIA: How do you read me?

HOUSTON: Columbia, he has landed Tranquility Base. Eagle is at Tranquility. I read you five by. Over.

COLUMBIA (the command and service module): Yes, I heard the whole thing.

HOUSTON: Well, it's a good show.

COLUMBIA: Fantastic.

TRANQUILITY BASE: I'll second that.

APOLLO CONTROL: The next major stay-no stay will be for the T2 event. That is at 21 minutes 26 seconds after initiation of power descent.

COLUMBIA: Up telemetry command reset to reacquire on high gain.

HOUSTON: Copy. Out.

APOLLO CONTROL: We have an unofficial time for that touchdown of 102 hours, 45 minutes, 42 seconds and we will update that.

HOUSTON: Eagle, you loaded R2 wrong. We want 10254.

TRANQUILITY BASE: Roger. Do you want the horizontal 55 15.2?

HOUSTON: That's affirmative.

APOLLO CONTROL: We're now less than four minutes from our next stay-no stay. It will be for one complete revolution of the command module.

One of the first things that Armstrong and Aldrin will do after getting their next stay-no stay will be to remove their helmets and gloves.

HOUSTON: Eagle, you are stay for T2. Over.

Continued on Page 4, Col. 1

VOYAGE TO THE MOON

By Archibald MacLeish

PRESENCE among us,
wonderer in our skies,

dazzle of silver in our leaves and on our
waters silver,

O
silver evasion in our farthest thought—
"the visiting moon" . . . "the glimpses of the moon" . . .

and we have touched you!

From the first of time,
before the first of time, before the
first men tasted time, we thought of you.
You were a wonder to us, unattainable,
a longing past the reach of longing,
a light beyond our light, our lives—perhaps
a meaning to us . . .

Now
our hands have touched you in your depth of night.

Three days and three nights we journeyed,
steered by farthest stars, climbed outward,
crossed the invisible tide-rip where the floating dust
falls one way or the other in the void between,
followed that other down, encountered
cold, faced death—unfathomable emptiness . . .

Then, the fourth day evening, we descended,
made fast, set foot at dawn upon your beaches,
sifted between our fingers your cold sand.

We stand here in the dusk, the cold, the silence . . .

and here, as at the first of time, we lift our heads.
Over us, more beautiful than the moon, a
moon, a wonder to us, unattainable,
a longing past the reach of longing,
a light beyond our light, our lives—perhaps
a meaning to us . . .

O, a meaning!

over us on these silent beaches the bright
earth,
presence among us

NEIL A. ARMSTRONG

EDWIN E. ALDRIN JR.

Associated Press

At Houston space center, screen at left showed touchdown of LM. Craft is represented by dot at screen's lower left.

Bleak, Rocky World Seen From Module

By JOHN NOBLE WILFORD

Special to The New York Times

HOUSTON, July 20—Man landed and walked on the moon today.

Two Americans, astronauts of Apollo 11, steered their fragile, four-legged lunar module safely and smoothly to the historic landing at 4:17:40 P.M., Eastern daylight time.

Neil A. Armstrong, the 38-year-old civilian commander, radioed to earth and the control room here:

"Houston, Tranquility Base here. The Eagle has landed."

The first men to reach the moon—Mr. Armstrong and his co-pilot, Col. Edwin E. Aldrin Jr. of the Air Force—brought their craft to rest on a level, rock-strewn plain near the southwestern shore of the arid Sea of Tranquility.

About six hours later, Mr. Armstrong opened the landing craft's hatch, stepped slowly down the ladder and planted the first human footprints on the lunar crust.

Outside their vehicle the astronauts found a bleak world. It was just after dawn, with the sun low over the eastern horizon behind them and the chill of the long lunar night still clinging to the boulders, small craters and hills before them.

Colonel Aldrin said that he could see "literally thousands of small craters" and a low hill out in the distance.

Crater Littered With Boulders

But most of all he was impressed initially by the "variety of shapes, angularities, granularities" of the rocks and soil where the landing craft, code-named Eagle, had set down.

The landing came about four miles west of the target point. The craft was steered past a crater littered with boulders on its approach.

As Eagle neared the surface of the moon, Mr. Armstrong saw that the computerized automatic pilot was sending the fragile ship toward the field scattered with rocks and boulders in the projected landing site on the moon's Sea of Tranquility.

He grabbed control of his ship, sent it clear of the area where it would have met almost certain disaster, and landed four miles beyond the original landing point.

It was a costly maneuver. It cut the available fuel short. When it landed, Eagle had barely 49 seconds worth of hovering rocket fuel left, less than half of the 114 seconds worth it was supposed to have.

Soon after the landing, upon checking and finding the spacecraft in good condition, Mr. Armstrong and Colonel Aldrin made their decision to open the hatch and get out more than five hours earlier than originally scheduled.

"Our recommendation at this point is planning EVA (Extra Vehicular Activity) with your concurrence starting at 8 o'clock this evening, Houston time [9 P.M., E.D.T.], about three hours from now," Mr. Armstrong radioed ground control.

"Tranquility Base, Houston. We've thought about it. We will support it," ground control replied.

Dramatic Triumph for Men

It was man's first landing on another world, the realization of centuries of dreams, the fulfillment of a decade of striving, a triumph of modern technology and personal courage, the most dramatic demonstration of what man can do if he applies his mind and resources with single-minded determination.

The moon, long the symbol of the impossible and the inaccessible, was now within man's reach, the first port of call in this new age of spacefaring.

Immediately after the landing, Dr. Thomas O. Paine, administrator of the National Aeronautics and Space Administration, telephoned President Nixon in Washington to report:

"Mr. President, it is my honor on behalf of the entire NASA team to report to you that the Eagle has landed on the Sea of Tranquility and our astronauts are safe and looking forward to starting the exploration of the moon."

The landing craft from the Apollo 11 spaceship was scheduled to remain on the moon about 22 hours, while Col. Michael Collins of the Air Force, the third member of the Apollo 11 crew, piloted the command ship, Columbia, in orbit overhead.

"You're looking good in every respect," Mission Con-

Continued on Page 3, Col. 1

Boulders May Prove Scientific Boons

By WALTER SULLIVAN

Special to The New York Times

HOUSTON, July 20 — Although the discovery that they were coming down in the middle of a boulder-filled moon crater may have given the two Apollo astronauts a few anxious moments today, it proved a scientific boon.

They managed to delay touchdown until they had skimmed across the crater, large as a football field, and beyond its rim, but they came down in an area that was strewn with boulders of many sizes and varieties.

Some were presumably blown out of the lunar depths when the crater was formed, representing rock buried perhaps 100 feet or more below the surface—far beyond the reach of the two men's sampling tools.

Other rocks probably were thrown from over the horizon by more massive impact and thus are specimens from other regions of the moon. Since the moon has virtually no air and its gravity is only one-sixth as strong as earth's gravity, explosive impacts sometimes blew debris halfway around the moon.

Furthermore, the boulders may make it possible to place the two scientific packages to be left on the moon so that they will be sheltered from dust thrown up by the blast of the lift-off rocket.

Such dust is probably the chief worry of those who have prepared the two packages. One is a small but highly sensitive seismic station.

Those who have long debated whether the moon is a dead body, with a cool interior and no volcanic activity, or is turbulent within, like the earth, are eagerly awaiting the data from this instrument.

They hope, from the four seismometers inside it, to distinguish between earthquakes generated within the moon, volcanic eruptions at the surface and meteorite impacts.

The unit is designed so that, when it has been set up on the moon and its folded panels open up in the glaring sunlight, the panels will begin to convert light into electricity. This initiates radio transmissions to the earth. Specialists here, by radio command, can then free the delicately suspended weights that can sense moon tremors.

Operation is dependent on the light-gathering panels "being

Continued on Page 3, Column 7

Luna Dips to 10 Miles From Moon; Surmises Soar

By BERNARD GWERTZMAN

Special to The New York Times

MOSCOW, July 20 — The Soviet Union announced tonight that the orbit of its unmanned spacecraft Luna 15 had again been altered, bringing it to within 10 miles of the moon's surface.

Tass, the Soviet press agency, made the disclosure only minutes before the Apollo 11 moon module detached from its mother ship on its historic attempt to land men on the moon and return them to earth.

The new elliptical orbit of Luna 15 created tension among observers here, who wondered if the latest correction was a prelude to an attempted lunar landing by the Russians, perhaps even in the same vicinity where the Americans were due to land.

Soviet officials have given assurances to the Americans that Luna 15 would not interfere with the Apollo mission. But the new orbit led to renewed speculation that the Russians might try to land the Luna craft and return it to earth with moon rock in an effort to demonstrate that unmanned craft were the equal of manned ships, if not more valuable.

As usual, Tass gave no information on the goal of Luna 15. It said only "the automatic station Luna 15 continues scientific exploration in the near-moon outer space."

Tass said that the latest maneuver took place at 5:16 P.M. Moscow time today (10:16 A.M. Eastern daylight time).

Luna 15 was launched last Sunday and went into moon orbit on Thursday. Last night Tass announced that its orbit had been altered to between 136 miles at the maximum and 50 miles at the minimum from the surface of the moon.

Today's correction brought the craft into an orbit of 68.3 miles maximum and 9.94 miles minimum.

The orbit's inclination to the plane of the lunar equator was given as 127 degrees, a slight change from yesterday's 126.

In its new orbit, Luna 15

Continued on Page 10, Column 3

Today's 4-Part Issue of The Times

This morning's issue of The New York Times is divided into four parts. The first part is devoted to news of Apollo 11, and includes Editorials and letters to the Editor (Page 18). Poems on the landing on the moon appear on Page 17.

General news begins on the first page of the second part. The News Summary and Index is on the first page of the third part, which includes sports news, obituaries (Page 51) and transportation news and weather reports (Pages 50 and 52).

Financial and business news begins on the first page of the fourth part.

Following is the News Index for today's issue:

The Cold War
A History in Documents

Allan M. Winkler

OXFORD
UNIVERSITY PRESS

For Karen Winkler Moulton

OXFORD
UNIVERSITY PRESS

Oxford New York

Auckland Bangkok Buenos Aries Cape Town Chennai
Dar es Salaam Delhi Hong Kong Istanbul Karachi Kolkata
Kuala Lumpur Madrid Melbourne Mexico City Mumbai Nairobi
São Paulo Shanghai Singapore Taipei Tokyo Toronto

Copyright © 2000 by Allan M. Winkler
First published as an Oxford paperback in 2003

Design: Sandy Kaufman
Layout: Loraine Machlin

Published by Oxford University Press, Inc.,
198 Madison Avenue, New York, New York 10016
www.oup.com

Library of Congress Cataloging-in-Publication Data
Winkler, Allan M.
The Cold War: a history in documents / Allan M. Winkler.
p. cm. — (Pages from history)
Includes bibliographical references and index.
Summary: Uses contemporary documents to explore the development of
the Cold War struggle, the consequences in the 1950s and 1960s, and the
lasting effects on American social and cultural patterns.
ISBN 0-19-512356-5 (hardcover) 0-19-516637-X (paperback)
1. Cold War—Sources. 2. World politics—1945—-Sources. 3. United
States—Foreign relations—Russia—Sources. 4. Russia—Foreign relations—
United States—Sources. [1. Cold War—Sources. 2. World politics—
1945—-Sources.] I. Title. II. Series.
D842 .W56 2000
909.8—dc21
00-027270

5 7 9 8 6 4

Printed in the United States of America
on acid-free paper

Cover: *Civil Defense drills in schools during the
1950s taught children to lie down with their
heads covered to prepare for a possible emergency.*

Frontispiece: *In 1969, the United States fulfilled President John F. Kennedy's promise to land
a man on the moon. Pictures transmitted from the
moon itself during the landing fascinated people
around the world.*

Title page: *A mushroom cloud from an atomic
bomb test at the Bikini atoll in the Pacific Ocean
in 1946.*

Contents

What Is a Document?

To the historian, a document is, quite simply, any sort of historical evidence. It is a primary source, the raw material of history. A document may be more than the expected government paperwork, such as a treaty or passport. It is also a letter, diary, will, grocery list, newspaper article, recipe, memoir, oral history, school yearbook, map, chart, architectural plan, poster, musical score, play script, novel, political cartoon, painting, photograph—even an object.

Using primary sources allows us not just to read *about* history, but to read history itself. It allows us to immerse ourselves in the look and feel of an era gone by, to understand its people and their language, whether verbal or visual. And it allows us to take an active, hands-on role in (re)constructing history.

Using primary sources requires us to use our powers of detection to ferret out the relevant facts and to draw conclusions from them; just as Agatha Christie uses the scores in a bridge game to determine the identity of a murderer, the historian uses facts from a variety of sources—some, perhaps, seemingly inconsequential—to build a historical case.

The poet W. H. Auden wrote that history was the study of questions. Primary sources force us to ask questions—and then, by answering them, to construct a narrative or an argument that makes sense to us. Moreover, as we draw on the many sources from "the dust-bin of history," we can endow that narrative with character, personality, and texture—all the elements that make history so endlessly intriguing.

Cartoon
This political cartoon addresses the issue of church and state. It illustrates the Supreme Court's role in balancing the demands of the First Amendment of the Constitution and the desires of the religious population.

Illustration
Illustrations from children's books, such as this alphabet from the New England Primer, tell us how children were educated, and also what the religious and moral values of the time were.

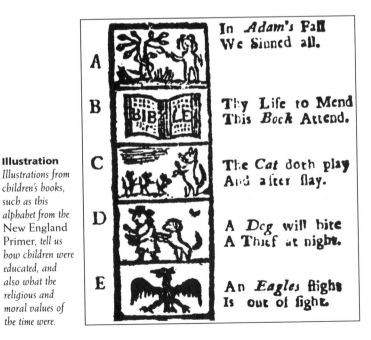

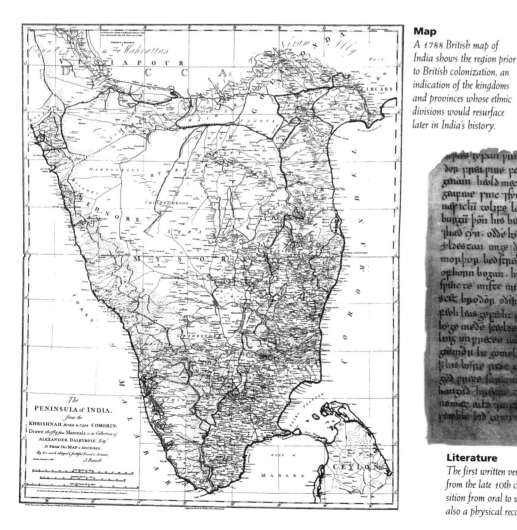

Map

A 1788 British map of India shows the region prior to British colonization, an indication of the kingdoms and provinces whose ethnic divisions would resurface later in India's history.

Treaty

A government document such as this 1805 treaty can reveal not only the details of government policy, but information about the people who signed it. Here, the Indians' names were written in English transliteration by U.S. officials; the Indians added pictographs to the right of their names.

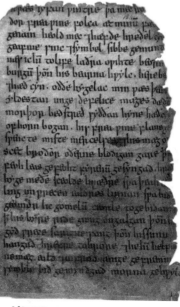

Literature

The first written version of the Old English epic Beowulf, from the late 10th century, is physical evidence of the transition from oral to written history. Charred by fire, it is also a physical record of the wear and tear of history.

How to Read a Document

Every document in this book relates to the bitter conflict between the United States and the Soviet Union that lasted for nearly half a century after World War II. The cold war was all consuming and affected not only political and diplomatic affairs but social and economic issues as well. Some of the documents in this collection come from government records; others come from the world of popular culture. All of them help us understand the origins and consequences of the struggle.

As you read this book, ask yourself about the source and message of each document. The same questions apply whether you are looking at a letter or a photograph or a cartoon: Who was the author and who was the intended audience? What was the creator of the document trying to say?

The cartoon and the photograph on the opposite page are examples of two kinds of cold war documents. They frame the period chronologically. Political cartoons often use humor or satire to make a point but may still have a serious message. The caricature from the early years of the cold war of Soviet leader Joseph Stalin standing on a pile of coffins shows how one artist viewed the ruthless efforts of the Soviet Union to control all of eastern Europe. American commentators often focused on Soviet repression and brutality in enforcing the communist party line, and this cartoon—with its hostile view of Stalin—is typical of many such images. The photograph from the end of the cold war of Russian leader Boris Yeltsin standing in front of the White House with President George Bush and his wife Barbara creates a much friendlier impression. No longer are the two leaders adversaries; now they appear as companions. Yeltsin's arms circle the Bushes, and with the dogs standing in front, this picture looks like it could be a family Christmas card to the world.

This book also includes many other less graphic documents, such as letters, telegrams, transcripts of government hearings, and popular songs. These provide a sense of what government leaders were thinking as they made crucial decisions, and of how ordinary people viewed the choices their leaders made. No one document can explain the period. Taken together, the documents can help us understand the dramatic confrontation that dominated the second half of the 20th century.

Caricature

Cartoonists often exaggerate certain features of the figure they are drawing. In this cartoon, the artist's rendering of Stalin's big, bushy mustache, his most prominent characteristic, indicates that this is without question the Soviet leader. Americans, who knew of the way Stalin liquidated his political opponents, believed that he would stop at nothing to achieve his ends, and the mustache and archly pointed eyebrows give the Soviet ruler a sinister look.

Symbols

The artist uses symbols to represent the issues under consideration. In this cartoon, the paper Stalin is holding titled "U.S. Aggression" represents the accusatory message he proclaimed to the rest of the world. The coffins piled high contain the names of various Eastern European countries the Soviet Union brought under its tight control. Americans worried about those nations trapped behind what British statesman Winston Churchill called the "iron curtain," and this cartoon reminds readers of their fate. Such symbols highlight the irony of Stalin accusing the United States of doing precisely what the Soviet Union had done.

Subject

This 1992 photograph shows Boris Yeltsin, President of Russia, standing with the American President and his wife in the aftermath of the cold war. As the Soviet Union fragmented into its component parts, Russia emerged as the most important of the republics and Yeltsin was the most influential leader in that part of the world. But now, instead of hostility, the Russian and American leaders show real friendliness toward one another. They appear open and relaxed, in shirtsleeves, without more formal suit jackets.

Interpretation

This photograph sends an important message to the world. The informality of the pose conveys the sense that relations between Russia and the United States are now comfortable, and the hostilities that lasted so long are now over. Yeltsin's arms encircling George and Barbara Bush make this seem like a family portrait, while the presence of the dogs, who were an important part of the Bush household, underscores this impression. At the same time, the location of the protagonists in front of the White House, home of the American President, emphasizes that this scene is unfolding on American turf, since the United States emerged victorious in the cold war.

Introduction

The cold war was a bitter, usually nonmilitary, conflict between the United States and the Soviet Union that lasted for almost 50 years after World War II. The struggle had its roots in long-standing disagreements between the two nations that dated back to the Russian Revolution of 1917. The Soviets and Americans set aside their differences in the early 1940s to fight together to defeat Adolf Hitler and the other Axis powers. But as World War II drew to a close in 1945, the old disputes resurfaced, with the cold war as the result.

The cold war was not a conventional conflict fought on traditional battlefields, yet it affected all aspects of American life. It provided the framework for all foreign policy initiatives and diplomatic decisions in the post–World War II years. Occasionally, tensions could not be contained and actual fighting broke out, as in the Korean War and the war in Vietnam. For the most part, though, military confrontations were avoided, leaving the underlying friction to surface in other ways. The cold war caused the growth of military arsenals on both sides and fueled a frightening arms race, which came to include nuclear weapons. It influenced virtually all budget decisions in that spending money for military programs abroad left correspondingly less for reform efforts at home. And it created a climate of fear that in the 1950s even threatened the internal stability of the United States.

The roots of the cold war lay deep in the past. Antagonisms arose when revolutionary Bolsheviks (the radical socialist majority party) in Russia overthrew the imperial ruler—the czar—and established their own state in 1917. Americans, who had reacted with concern to radical uprisings in Europe in 1830 and 1848, were even more troubled by the establishment of the huge new Soviet Union that seemed to challenge the democratic values of the United States. Particularly bothersome was the new communist country's commitment to a world order led by workers and its rejection of organized

Americans were overjoyed when World War II finally came to an end in 1945. They had made considerable sacrifices during the struggle, and were ready to enjoy the peace and prosperity for which they had fought. Here they congregate on Pennsylvania Avenue in front of the White House in Washington, D.C., to celebrate Japan's surrender.

Note written by P.M during conversation with Marshal Stalin at the Kremlin 9.10.44. Attached is interpreter's translation. (Red ink added later).

Roumania

Russia 90%

the others 10%

Greece (Great Britain) (in accord with U.S.A.) 90%

the others / Russia 10%

Yugoslavia 50/50

W.S.C.

Hungary 50/50

Bulgaria Russia 75% / the others 25%

The United States, Great Britain, and the Soviet Union were allies during World War II and met at a number of conferences to plan strategy. At a meeting with Soviet Premier Joseph Stalin in Moscow in 1944, British Prime Minister Winston Churchill suggested the postwar division of various countries into spheres of influence, which Stalin approved by making check marks on the page. In Romania, for example, the Russians would have 90% control and the Allies would have 10%.

religion. U.S. President Woodrow Wilson, worried about the influence of Bolshevik leader Vladimir Ilyich Lenin on downtrodden people in other parts of the world, sent U.S. troops to Russia in 1919 to try to defeat the revolutionaries. When that effort failed, the United States refused to grant the new regime formal diplomatic recognition, and the result was an uneasy stalemate that lasted until 1933, when President Franklin D. Roosevelt accepted the futility of the nonrecognition policy and established diplomatic ties. Some Americans, weary of the Great Depression that was devastating the U.S.—and the world—economy, looked to the Soviet Union as the model of a new world order. Others remained suspicious of the communist state.

The antagonism intensified in 1939, when Soviet leader Joseph Stalin signed a nonaggression pact with German chancellor Hitler. But the Russians turned from enemies into friends after Hitler attacked the Soviet Union in 1941. As the United States, Great Britain, and the Soviet Union fought together within the Grand Alliance, Americans began to view Stalin and the Soviet state with far more sympathy. Russians suppressed their commitment to the overthrow of the capitalist world; Americans now viewed their former antagonists as friendly people just like them.

As World War II came to an end in 1945, disagreements that had only been suppressed surfaced once more. The United States emerged from the war strong and secure, eager to spread its vision of freedom and economic opportunity around the world. Americans believed in the principles of liberty, equality, and opportunity that had governed the nation for nearly 200 years and wanted to spread them to all parts of the globe. The Soviet Union, on the other hand, was concerned first with its own security after a devastating war in which 20 million of its people had died. The Russians wanted to rebuild at home, with friendly neighbors on their western flank, through which they had been invaded at various points in the past. As Soviet and American aims came into conflict, the cold war began. The issues that caused the greatest antagonism and the confrontations that occurred at regular intervals in the post–World War II years unfold in detail in the following pages.

The arms race was one result of the international competition. Although many soldiers returned home at the war's end, the United States maintained its military strength even as it began to rely more and more on nuclear weapons. The dramatic demonstrations in 1945 of the impact of the atomic bomb on Hiroshima and Nagasaki in Japan provided a first glimpse at the awesome new force that had been unleashed. In the 1950s, scientists created new thermonuclear weapons—hydrogen bombs—that were far more powerful than atomic bombs. These weapons now became the bargaining chips in an arms race more deadly than any in the past. At the same time, the United States and the Soviet Union began to compete in space as well, launching satellites such as the Russian *Sputnik* ("fellow traveler," of Earth) that circled the globe in 1957. This Soviet technological achievement was embarrassing enough, but the United States was even more worried that the guided missiles necessary to launch a satellite into orbit could also deliver hydrogen bombs.

Meanwhile, the arms race encouraged an alliance between government and business, known as the military-industrial complex, that built military hardware while enriching defense contractors and stimulating extraordinary economic growth. As columnist David Lawrence observed in 1950, "Government planners figure they have found the magic formula for almost endless good times. Cold War is the catalyst. Cold War is an economic pump primer. Turn a spigot, and the public clamors for more arms spending." Thanks to such expenditures, the post–World War II years were tremendously prosperous. The Gross National Product (GNP)—the total annual goods and services produced—soared from just over $200 billion in 1945 to almost $300 billion in 1950 and to more than $500 billion in 1960. U.S. consumers, who had suffered through the deprivations of the Great Depression in the 1930s and then shortages of things they wanted because of the priorities of military production in the early 1940s, were now ready to acquire whatever they could. They purchased cars and homes and household appliances in a frenzy of buying activity that promoted the continuing expansion of the economy.

Most American women were home-makers in the early years of the cold war. They married young, took care of their children, and did all of the housework, often with the assistance of bigger and better labor-saving devices like the washer and dryer pictured in this Maytag ad.

The cold war, however, affected more than military, diplomatic, and economic affairs. It also had a pronounced effect on social patterns. Family life, for example, reflected the impact of the new peacetime struggle. Many women, who had worked in factories making weapons of war during World War II, now found themselves forced to return to the home in the 1950s as Americans reaffirmed the traditional roles of men and women that had prevailed before the war. A woman's place was in the kitchen, her role to take care of the children who were part of a huge baby boom. As author Betty Friedan wrote in 1963 in *The Feminine Mystique*, a scathing critique of the social patterns of the 1950s, women "could desire no greater destiny than to glory in their own femininity. . . . All they had to do was to devote their lives from earliest girlhood to finding a husband and bearing children." Continuing with her assessment, she observed that "it was unquestioned gospel that women could identify with *nothing* beyond the home—not politics, not art, not science, not events large or small, war or peace, in the United States or the world, unless it could be approached through female experience as a wife or mother or translated into domestic detail." The culture said that women needed to do their part to support America in the cold war by adhering to traditional patterns. By playing a maternal role, they supported strong families that could be a bulwark against the communist menace.

The cold war was likewise intertwined with the intensifying struggle for civil rights. As African Americans challenged the system of segregation separating blacks and whites by filing court cases and staging boycotts and other demonstrations, government officials worried about how such domestic upheavals might be perceived abroad. With the international press covering lynchings and other reflections of racism, it was clear that racial discrimination posed an obstacle to the campaign to enlist allies in large parts of the world. Though the cold war was hardly the most important factor in the campaign for equality, it nevertheless helped advance the cause of domestic reform.

In the same way, the cold war helped spark the cultural upheaval of the 1960s. As the war in Vietnam tore the United

States apart and millions of young Americans mobilized against the actions of their own government, traditional political configurations began to shift. While radicals spoke about the need for a New Left, the liberal Democratic party faced an even greater challenge from the conservative Republican party, which started to play an increasingly important political role. Meanwhile, other Americans, drawn by the call of the counterculture, dropped out of traditional society altogether.

This book tries to capture the most important cross-currents of the cold war, which ended only in the last decade of the 20th century. With the conflict finally over, it is now possible to look with greater perspective at the issues and events that preoccupied people for so long at home and abroad. Using both public and private documents generated by the protagonists themselves, this book charts the course of U.S. policy in the half century after World War II and describes the most serious confrontations that occurred. While it examines numerous decisions and their consequences, it is not a history of everything that unfolded in the postwar period, but rather a focused assessment of the most visible, direct effects of the long-lasting confrontation that had such a powerful impact on both the Soviet Union and the United States.

Members of the National Association for the Advancement of Colored People (NAACP) march to the Florida state capitol in Tallahassee. The NAACP played a central role in the civil rights revolution of the 1950s and 1960s, protesting violence against blacks, challenging racist laws in the courts, and lobbying for fair employment opportunities and voting rights.

Chapter One

Early Antagonism

The cold war developed out of international tensions that had been suppressed during World War II. The three major Allies—the United States, Great Britain, and the Soviet Union—had their own national aims and priorities in the war, but they managed for the most part to smooth over their differences in order to defeat the Axis powers—Germany, Italy, and Japan. Sometimes, however, disagreements surfaced among the Allies even before the final victory was won, and friction between them became more visible by the end of the war.

Leaders of the Big Three met at a series of wartime conferences to settle questions of strategy and to determine the shape of the postwar world. United States President Franklin D. Roosevelt enjoyed a close relationship with British Prime Minister Winston Churchill and sought to use his charm to reassure Soviet leader Joseph Stalin that the major powers were working together toward a common end. These key figures made compromises on most major issues in conferences at Teheran, in modern-day Iran, in December 1943; at Yalta, in the Crimea (today's Ukraine) in February 1945; and at Potsdam, in Germany, in July 1945, where Harry S. Truman replaced Roosevelt, who had recently died.

Despite a superficial consensus about when to launch a European invasion and what to do about Poland and Germany after the war, each major power remained well aware of differences that could not be entirely ignored. The Soviet Union sought a quick strike on the European continent, to ease pressure on its borders, where it was fighting the Germans without Allied support. But the British, remembering the brutal trench fighting of World War I, were reluctant to launch such an invasion until they felt certain it could succeed. The United States, caught in the middle, ended up accepting a policy of delay.

The Big Three also found themselves split over the creation of the atomic bomb. The United States worked with Britain in the program

British Prime Minister Winston Churchill, American President Harry S. Truman, and Soviet Premier Joseph Stalin met at Potsdam, Germany, in July 1945, at the end of the war in Europe, and demanded the unconditional surrender of the Japanese. At this meeting, Truman hinted to Stalin that the United States now had a new weapon of incredible explosive force, but he never identified the atomic bomb by name.

I made one great mistake in my life, when I signed the letter to President Roosevelt recommending that atom bombs be made, but there was some justification—the danger that the Germans would make them.

—Albert Einstein, after World War II, in a conversation with Linus Pauling

that came to be known as the Manhattan Project, but it treated Britain as a junior partner and never informed its ally the Soviet Union about this $2 billion initiative until the bomb was almost ready to be used. Meanwhile, as Soviet spies reported back to Stalin about the progress of the project, his awareness of what was happening only accentuated the growing rift.

Origin of the Atomic Bomb

After experiments in 1938 succeeded in splitting the nucleus of a uranium atom, scientists around the world speculated about the possibilities of atomic energy. They thought that, if this splitting, or fission, could be made to occur quickly, tremendous amounts of energy locked inside atoms might be released. Italian physicist Enrico Fermi theorized that this kind of bomb might be capable of destroying an entire city.

```
                                        Albert Einstein
                                        Old Grove Rd.
                                        Nassau Point
                                        Peconic, Long Island

                                        August 2nd, 1939

    F.D. Roosevelt,
    President of the United States,
    White House
    Washington, D.C.

    Sir:

          Some recent work by E.Fermi and L. Szilard, which has been com-
    municated to me in manuscript, leads me to expect that the element uran-
    ium may be turned into a new and important source of energy in the im-
    mediate future. Certain aspects of the situation which has arisen seem
    to call for watchfulness and, if necessary, quick action on the part
    of the Administration. I believe therefore that it is my duty to bring
    to your attention the following facts and recommendations:

          In the course of the last four months it has been made probable -
    through the work of Joliot in France as well as Fermi and Szilard in
    America - that it may become possible to set up a nuclear chain reaction
    in a large mass of uranium,by which vast amounts of power and large quant.
    ities of new radium-like elements would be generated. Now it appears
    almost certain that this could be achieved in the immediate future.

          This new phenomenon would also lead to the construction of bombs,
    and it is conceivable - though much less certain - that extremely power-
    ful bombs of a new type may thus be constructed. A single bomb of this
    type, carried by boat and exploded in a port, might very well destroy
    the whole port together with some of the surrounding territory. However,
    such bombs might very well prove to be too heavy for transportation by
    air.
```

Other scientists became even more concerned, fearing that Germany might be trying to create such a bomb. On the very eve of World War II, some of these scientists approached Albert Einstein, the physicist who had formulated the theory of relativity, to seek his help. Years before, as he worked on relativity, he had defined the formula $E=mc^2$ (energy is equal to mass multiplied by the speed of light squared), which suggested that matter and energy were equivalent. Now he was asked to sign a letter to President Roosevelt warning him about the kind of bomb that could now be created.

This letter helped launch the Manhattan Project and create the atomic bombs that helped bring an end to the war. Atomic energy became a powerful force entwined with the politics of the cold war. Einstein, however, troubled by what had occurred, later observed that atomic energy changed everything except our ways of thinking.

The United States has only very poor ores of uranium in moderate quantities. There is some good ore in Canada and the former Czechoslovakia, while the most important source of uranium is Belgian Congo.

In view of this situation you may think it desirable to have some permanent contact maintained between the Administration and the group of physicists working on chain reactions in America. One possible way of achieving this might be for you to entrust with this task a person who has your confidence and who could perhaps serve in an inofficial capacity. His task might comprise the following:

    a) to approach Government Departments, keep them informed of the further development, and put forward recommendations for Government action giving particular attention to the problem of securing a supply of uranium ore for the United States;

    b) to speed up the experimental work,which is at present being carried on within the limits of the budgets of University laboratories, by providing funds, if such funds be required, through his contacts with private persons who are willing to make contributions for this cause, and perhaps also by obtaining the co-operation of industrial laboratories which have the necessary equipment.

I understand that Germany has actually stopped the sale of uranium from the Czechoslovakian mines which she has taken over. That she should have taken such early action might perhaps be understood on the ground that the son of the German Under-Secretary of State, von Weizsäcker, is attached to the Kaiser-Wilhelm-Institut in Berlin where some of the American work on uranium is now being repeated.

Yours very truly,
A. Einstein
(Albert Einstein)

Soviet Foreign Minister Vyacheslav Molotov was the diplomat who frequently conveyed his government's position on cold war issues to the United States and reported back the American response.

Soon after becoming President in April 1945, Harry Truman met with Vyacheslav Molotov and scolded him for breaking agreements made at Yalta about the future fate of Europe. "I have never been talked to like that in my life," Molotov said angrily. "Carry out your agreements and you won't get talked to like that," Truman responded bluntly.

Tensions and Strategies

This cartoon appeared a week after Stalin's speech in February 1946, which ended his collaborative approach and predicted the inevitable victory of communism over capitalism. Stalin, called "Uncle Joe" here, appears as a cheerful artist, painting pictures with both hands. One picture portrays an angel with a globe head labeled "World Unity." The other portrays a devil with a globe head labeled "World Capitalism."

As World War II came to an end, the Soviet Union and the United States disagreed about how such nations as Poland and Germany should be treated after the war. These disagreements became increasingly difficult to resolve. Positions hardened, and sometimes the Allies appeared irritated with one another. They became even more confrontational in the first postwar years. In February 1946, Joseph Stalin gave a speech lashing out at the Western powers and proclaimed his confidence in the eventual triumph of the Soviet system. The Marxist ideology preaching the inevitable triumph of socialism—a system of government in which the national government owns all the means of production—had been toned down during the war in the interest of maintaining harmony among the Allies, but once the war was over, it reemerged in full force. Stalin argued that capitalism and communism were on a collision course and a series of terrible crises would tear the capitalist world apart. U.S. Supreme Court Justice William O. Douglas considered his speech to be a declaration of World War III.

Our Marxists declare that the capitalist system of world economy conceals elements of crisis and war, that the development of world capitalism does not follow a steady and even course forward, but proceeds through crises and catastrophes. The uneven development of the capitalist countries leads in time to sharp disturbances in their relations, and the group of countries which consider themselves inadequately provided with raw materials and export markets try usually to change this situation and to change the position in their favor by means of armed force.

As a result of these factors, the capitalist world is sent into two hostile camps and war follows. . . .

As far as our country is concerned, this war was the most cruel and hard of all wars ever experienced in the history of our motherland. But the war has not only been a curse; it was at the same time a hard school of trial and a testing of all the people's forces. . . .

Now victory means, first of all, that our Soviet social system has won, that the Soviet social system has successfully stood the test in the fire of war and has proved its complete vitality.

As is well known the assertion often has been made in the foreign press that the Soviet social system is a risky experiment,

Winston Churchill delivered an unequivocal declaration of the cold war in his speech at Westminster College in March 1946. Truman (seated, with academic cap) and other members of his administration were on the stage as Churchill warned listeners—and people around the world—of the Soviet-built "iron curtain" descending across the continent of Europe.

doomed to failure, that the Soviet system is a house of cards, without roots in real life, and imposed on the people by the organs of the Cheka [secret police] . . .

Now we can say that the war has refuted all the assertions of the foreign press as without foundation. The war has shown that the Soviet social system is a truly popular system, issued from the depths of the people and enjoying its mighty support. . . .

The point is that the Soviet social system has proved to be more capable of life and more stable than a non-Soviet social system, that the Soviet social system is a better form of organization of society than any non-Soviet social system. . . .

About a month after Stalin's speech, in March 1946, former British Prime Minister Winston Churchill responded to it. Speaking at Westminster College in Fulton, Missouri, with President Truman implicitly lending his approval by appearing on the platform with him, Churchill issued a ringing denunciation of the Soviet state and called for an ever-vigilant association of English-speaking peoples to work together to contain the Soviets' designs. His use of the term "iron curtain" became part of the vocabulary of the cold war.

When American military men approach some serious situation they are wont to write at the head of their directive the words

Harry Truman's Democratic party was proud of the way the United States was cooperating with Great Britain in the early years of the cold war. This campaign pin hailed that cooperative approach.

A Firm Stance

Most Americans agreed with Churchill's assessment of the Soviet threat. Even former Secretary of Commerce Henry A. Wallace, who was more sympathetic to the Soviet Union than many in the government, observed, "I think we can make it clear to the Soviet government that no country however powerful in a military or economic way can dominate by mere force over Eastern Europe and get away with it any more than we could in Latin America or England in India and Africa."

"Over-all strategic concept." There is wisdom in this as it leads to clarity of thought. What, then, is the over-all strategic concept which we should inscribe today? It is nothing less than the safety and welfare, the freedom and progress of all the homes and families of all the men and women in all the lands. . . .

To give security to these countless homes they must be shielded from the two gaunt marauders—war and tyranny. . . .

A world organization [the United Nations] has already been erected for the prime purpose of preventing war. . . .

I come now to the second danger which threatens the cottage home and ordinary people, namely tyranny. We cannot be blind to the fact that the liberties enjoyed by individual citizens throughout the United States and British empire are not valid in a considerable number of countries, some of which are very powerful. In these states control is enforced upon the common people by various kinds of all-embracing police governments, to a degree which is overwhelming and contrary to every principle of democracy. . . .

Neither the sure prevention of war, nor the continuous rise of world organizations, will be gained without what I have called the fraternal association of the English-speaking peoples. This means a special relationship between the British Commonwealth and Empire and the United States. . . .

From Stettin in the Baltic to Trieste in the Adriatic, an iron curtain has descended across the continent. Behind that line lie all the capitals of the ancient states of central and eastern Europe. Warsaw, Berlin, Prague, Vienna, Budapest, Belgrade, Bucharest, and Sofia, all these famous cities and the populations around them lie in the Soviet sphere and all are subject, in one form or another, not only to Soviet influence but to a very high and increasing measure of control from Moscow. . . .

From what I have seen of our Russian friends and allies during the war, I am convinced that there is nothing they admire so much as strength, and there is nothing for which they have less respect than for military weakness. For that reason the old doctrine of a balance of power is unsound. We cannot afford, if we can help it, to work on narrow margins, offering temptations to a trial of strength. If the western democracies stand together in strict adherence to the principles of the United Nations Charter, their influence for furthering these principles will be immense and no one is likely to molest them. If, however, they become divided or falter in their duty, and if these all-important years are allowed to slip away, then indeed catastrophe may overwhelm us all.

As the rhetoric escalated, U.S. policy makers began to consider how they might respond to the Soviet threat. George F. Kennan was the chargé d'affaires (second ranking officer) in the U.S. embassy in Moscow. In response to Stalin's speech, he sent off an 8,000-word cable, or telegram, to the State Department. In it he defined Soviet aims and aspirations and argued that Soviet aggression had to be checked at every turn.

Part 1: Basic Features of Post War Soviet Outlook, as Put Forward by Official Propaganda Machine. . .

(a) USSR still lives in antagonistic "capitalist encirclement" with which in the long run there can be no permanent peaceful coexistence. . . .

(b) Capitalist world is beset with internal conflicts, inherent in nature of capitalist society. . . .

(c) Internal conflicts of capitalism inevitably generate wars. . . .

(d) Intervention against USSR, while it would be disastrous to those who undertook it, would cause renewed delay in progress of Soviet socialism and must therefore be forestalled at all costs. . . .

(e) Conflicts between capitalist states, though likewise fraught with danger for USSR, nevertheless hold out great possibilities for advancement of socialist cause, particularly if USSR remains militarily powerful, ideologically monolithic and faithful to its present brilliant leadership. . . .

Part 2: Background of Outlook. . .

At bottom of Kremlin's neurotic view of world affairs is traditional and instinctive Russian sense of insecurity. Originally, this was insecurity of a peaceful agricultural people trying to live on vast exposed plain in neighborhood of fierce nomadic peoples. To this was added, as Russia came into contact with economically advanced West, fear of more competent, more powerful, more highly organized societies in that area. But this latter type of insecurity was one which afflicted rather Russian rulers than Russian people; for Russian rulers have invariably sensed that their rule was relatively archaic in form, fragile and artificial in its psychological foundation, unable to stand comparison or contact with

The "long telegram" George Kennan sent from the Soviet Union to the U.S. Department of State in February 1946 shocked policy makers in the United States. From the first page, shown here, to the very end, the telegram helped shape the policy of containment that guided the United States during the cold war.

Reflecting on his telegram a year later, Kennan wrote, "I was conscious of the weakness of the Russian position, of the slenderness of the means with which they operated, of the ease with which they could be held and pushed back."

political systems of Western countries. For this reason, they have always feared foreign penetration, feared direct contact between Western world and their own, feared what would happen if Russians learned truth about world without or if foreigners learned truth about world within. And they have learned to seek security only in patient but deadly struggle for total destruction of rival power, never in compacts or compromises with it. . . .

Basically this is only the steady advance of uneasy Russian nationalism, a centuries old movement in which conceptions of offense and defense are inextricably confused. But in new guise of international Marxism, with its honeyed promises to a desperate and war torn outside world, it is more dangerous and insidious than ever before. . . .

Part 5: Practical deductions from Standpoint of U.S. Policy

In summary, we have here a political force committed fanatically to the belief that with U.S. there can be no further *modus vivendi* [means of getting along], that it is desirable and necessary that the internal harmony of our society be disrupted, our traditional way of life be destroyed, the international authority of our state be broken, if Soviet power is to be secure. . . .

Soviet power. . . does not work by fixed plans. It does not take unnecessary risks. Impervious to logic, it is highly sensitive to logic of force. For this reason it can easily withdraw—and usually does—when strong resistance is encountered at any point. . . .

Gauged against Western World as a whole, Soviets are still by far the weaker force. Thus, their success will really depend on degree of cohesion, firmness and vigor which Western World can muster. And this is factor which it is within our power to influence. . . .

Diplomats at home were impressed with Kennan's analysis. Soon Kennan found himself reassigned to a more influential position in the State Department, where he helped influence the direction of U.S. foreign policy. The year after his long telegram, in 1947, he published an important article in the influential journal *Foreign Affairs*. Writing under the pseudonym "Mr. X," because he was reluctant to have his essay appear to be an official government statement, he again analyzed the roots of Soviet conduct and argued that it was necessary to contain Soviet threats against any part of the world. His image of Russian policy as being like a "persistent

toy automobile wound up and headed in a given direction, stopping only when it meets with some unanswerable force" was widely quoted in assessments of Soviet demands. Kennan's concept of containment of the Soviet Union within existing boundaries became the theoretical justification for U.S. policy in the cold war.

The political personality of Soviet power as we know it today is the product of ideology and circumstances: ideology inherited by the present Soviet leaders from the movement in which they had their political origin, and circumstances of the power which they now have exercised for nearly three decades in Russia. . . .

The circumstances of the immediate post-Revolution period—the existence in Russia of civil war and foreign intervention, together with the obvious fact that the Communists represented only a tiny minority of the Russian people—made the establishment of dictatorial power a necessity. . . .

And within the [Communist] Party the same principle [of dictatorship] was to apply. The mass of Party members might go through the motions of election, deliberation, decision and action; but in these motions they were to be animated not by their own individual wills but by the awesome breath of the Party leadership. . .

Now it lies in the nature of the mental world of the Soviet leaders, as well as in the character of their ideology, that no opposition to them can be officially recognized as having any merit or justification whatsoever. . . .

So much for the historical background. What does it spell in terms of the political personality of Soviet power as we know it today?

Of the original ideology, nothing has been officially junked. Belief is maintained in the basic badness of capitalism, in the inevitability of its destruction, in the obligation of the proletariat [the working class] to assist in that destruction and to take power into its own hands. But stress has come to be laid primarily on those concepts which relate most specifically to the Soviet regime itself: to its position as the sole truly Socialist regime in a dark and misguided world, and to the relationships of power within it. . . .

The accumulative effect of these factors [the conflict between capitalism and communism, and the claimed infallibility of the Communist Party] is to give to the whole subordinate apparatus of Soviet power an unshakeable stubbornness and steadfastness in

Not everyone agreed with Kennan's analysis of the Soviet outlook. Journalist Walter Lippmann argued that the historical pattern of Russian efforts to expand was more important than communist ideology in molding Soviet policy: "Stalin is not only the heir of Marx [one of the authors of the *Communist Manifesto*] and of Lenin [first leader of the communist state] but of Peter the Great, the Czar of all the Russians."

In his article in Foreign Affairs, *George Kennan referred to the well-known logo for RCA records, entitled "His Master's Voice." The logo was based on this 1899 painting of a dog listening intently to the voice of his master playing on a gramophone. Kennan was suggesting that communists did not think for themselves but blindly followed the dictates of their master.*

its orientation. The orientation can be changed at will by the Kremlin [the Soviet government] but by no other power. Once a given party line has been laid down on a given issue of current policy, the whole Soviet governmental machine, including the mechanism of diplomacy, moves inexorably along the prescribed path, like a persistent toy automobile wound up and headed in a given direction, stopping only when it meets with some unanswerable force. The individuals of this machine are unamenable to argument or reason which comes to them from outside sources. Their whole training has taught them to mistrust and discount the glib persuasiveness of the outside world. Like the white dog before the phonograph [in an advertisement for RCA Victor records a decade before], they hear only the "master's voice." And if they are to be called off from the purposes last dictated to them, it is the master who must call them off. . . .

These considerations make Soviet diplomacy at once easier and more difficult to deal with than the diplomacy of individual aggressive leaders like Napoleon and Hitler. On the one hand it is more sensitive to contrary force, more ready to yield on individual sectors of the diplomatic front when that force is felt to be too strong, and thus more rational in the logic and rhetoric of power. On the other hand it cannot be easily defeated or discouraged by a single victory on the part of its opponents. . . .

In these circumstances it is clear that the main element of any United States policy toward the Soviet Union must be that of a long-term, patient but firm and vigilant containment of Russian expansive tendencies. . . .

It would be an exaggeration to say that American behavior unassisted and alone could exercise a power of life and death over the Communist movement and bring about the early fall of Soviet power in Russia. But the United States has it in its power to increase enormously the strains under which Soviet policy must operate, to force upon the Kremlin a far greater degree of moderation and circumspection than it has had to observe in recent years, and in this way to promote tendencies which must eventually find their outlet in either the breakup or the gradual mellowing of Soviet power. . . .

The Truman Doctrine

Meanwhile, external events led the United States to resist what it regarded as Soviet incursions into other parts of the world in just the way Kennan demanded. In the aftermath of

World War II, the Soviet Union sought to force Turkey into allowing joint control of the Dardanelles, the passage of water leading from the Russian-controlled Black Sea out to the Mediterranean Sea. At the same time, a civil war in Greece pitted communist forces against the right-wing monarchy supported by the British government. In February 1947, the British ambassador to the United States told the U.S. State Department that his country, devastated by the war, could no longer provide Greece and Turkey with economic and military aid. He asked for American assistance in moving into the expected void.

The Truman administration began to debate about what to do. Policy makers knew that a conservative Congress wanted to trim the budget and cut taxes, rather than craft new and expensive foreign aid programs. But they also recognized the need to assist nations threatened by the Soviet Union that might not survive without help. On March 12, 1947, Truman gave a speech in which he called on Congress to assist free peoples everywhere who were resisting subjugation, and specifically asked legislators to appropriate aid for Greece and Turkey. To avert the calamity that he feared, he requested Congress to authorize $400 million for such assistance. Congress complied, and the Truman Doctrine was the result.

The gravity of the situation which confronts the world today necessitates my appearance before a joint session of the Congress.

The foreign policy and the national security of this country are involved.

One aspect of the present situation, which I wish to present to you at this time for your consideration and decision, concerns Greece and Turkey.

The United States has received from the Greek Government an urgent appeal for financial and economic assistance. Preliminary reports from the American Economic Mission now in Greece and reports from the American Ambassador in Greece corroborate the statement of the Greek Government that assistance is imperative if Greece is to survive as a free nation. . . .

The very existence of the Greek state is today threatened by the terrorist activities of several thousand armed men, led by Communists, who defy the Government's authority at a number of points, particularly along the northern boundaries. . . .

Greece must have assistance if it is to become a self-supporting and self-respecting democracy.

The United States must supply that assistance. We have already extended to Greece certain types of relief and economic aid, but these are inadequate.

There is no other country to which democratic Greece can turn.

No other nation is willing and able to provide the necessary support for a democratic Greek government. . . .

Greece's neighbor, Turkey, also deserves our attention.

The future of Turkey as an independent and economically sound state is clearly no less important to the freedom-loving peoples of the world than the future of Greece. The circumstances in which Turkey finds itself today are considerably different from those of Greece. Turkey has been spared the disasters that have beset Greece. And during the war the United States and Great Britain furnished Turkey with material aid.

Nevertheless, Turkey now needs our support.

Since the war, Turkey has sought additional financial assistance from Great Britain and the United States for the purpose of effecting that modernization necessary for the maintenance of its national integrity.

That integrity is essential to the preservation of order in the Middle East. . . .

As in the case of Greece, if Turkey is to have the assistance it needs, the United States must supply it. We are the only country able to provide that help. . . .

At the present moment in world history nearly every nation must choose between alternative ways of life. The choice is too often not a free one.

One way of life is based upon the will of the majority, and is distinguished by free institutions, representative government, free elections, guaranties of individual liberty, freedom of speech and religion, and freedom from political oppression.

The second way of life is based upon the will of the minority forcibly imposed upon the majority. It relies upon terror and oppression, a controlled press and radio, fixed elections, and the suppression of personal freedoms.

I believe that it must be the policy of the United States to support free peoples who are resisting attempted subjugation by armed minorities or by outside pressures.

I believe that we must assist free peoples to work out their own destinies in their own way. . . .

Great responsibilities have been placed upon us by the swift movement of events.

In the past eighteen months, I said, Soviet pressure on the Straits [the Dardanelles], on Iran, and on northern Greece had brought the Balkans to the point where a highly possible Soviet breakthrough might open three continents to Soviet penetration. Like apples in a barrel infected by one rotten one, the corruption of Greece would affect Iran and all to the east.

—Under Secretary of State Dean Acheson, recalling a White House meeting with congressional leaders to discuss the need to assist Greece and Turkey

Mr. President, if you will say that to the Congress and the country, I will support you and I believe that most of its members will do the same.

—Sen. Arthur Vandenberg's response to President Truman after Under Secretary Acheson's statement

Both Great Britain and the United States worried about Greek guerrilla fighters who were challenging the established government in Greece in 1947. When the British could no longer afford to assist the government forces, the United States provided the necessary aid through what came to be called the Truman Doctrine.

I am confident that the Congress will face these responsibilities squarely.

The Marshall Plan

The next step came later in 1947. Europe desperately needed economic aid after the devastation of World War II. U.S. policy makers worried about economic and political instability that would open the way to communist domination in many nations there. In France and Italy, for example, communist parties were already growing stronger, causing problems for established governments. Following a foreign ministers' conference in Moscow, Secretary of State George C. Marshall returned to the United States and reported that Western Europe needed immediate help. "The patient is sinking while the doctors deliberate," he said.

The U.S. business community was sympathetic to a program of assistance that might create added markets overseas. American industry was booming, and needed more customers to avert the kind of downturn that had occurred after World War I.

Marshall unveiled the Truman administration's thinking at the Harvard University commencement in June 1947. Though most policy makers in the United States and Europe applauded the initiative, some critics opposed the proposal. Former Secretary of Commerce Henry A. Wallace, fearing it

This Generation's
Chance for Peace

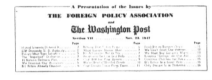

The European Recovery Program

'The Marshall Plan'

A Presentation of the Issues by
THE FOREIGN POLICY ASSOCIATION
and
The Washington Post

Secretary of State George C. Marshall, the army chief of staff responsible for the Allied victory during World War II, was worried that economic instability in Europe would lead to the triumph of communism. He proposed the massive economic aid program that came to be known as the Marshall Plan to ensure that the European nations that had survived the war would not fall to another foe.

Grim Prophecy

If the countries of middle-western and Mediterranean Europe sink under the burden of despair and become Communist, Scandinavia will fall into the same camp. The strategically and economically vital North African and middle-eastern areas will follow. This transfer of Western Europe, the second greatest industrial area in the world, and of the essential regions which must inevitably follow such a lead, would radically change the American position. If it should prove that a weakened United Kingdom could not resist so powerful a current, the shift would be cataclysmic.

—Secretary of Commerce Averell Harriman, agreeing with George C. Marshall's analysis of the crisis in Europe

would lead to further tensions between Soviets and Americans, called what came to be known as the Marshall Plan the Martial Plan instead.

I need not tell you gentlemen that the world situation is very serious. That must be apparent to all intelligent people. I think one difficulty is that the problem is one of such enormous complexity that the very mass of facts presented to the public and radio make it extremely difficult for the man in the street to reach a clear appraisement [appraisal] of the situation. Furthermore, the people of this country are distant from the troubled areas of the earth and it is hard for them to comprehend the plight and consequent reactions of the long-suffering peoples, and the effect of those reactions on their own governments in connection with our efforts to promote peace in the world.

In considering the requirements for the rehabilitation of Europe, the physical loss of life, the visible destruction of cities, factories, mines, and railroads was correctly estimated, but it has become obvious during recent months that this visible destruction was probably less serious than the dislocation of the entire fabric of [the] European economy. For the past 10 years conditions have been highly abnormal. The feverish preparation for war and the more feverish maintenance of the war effort engulfed all aspects of national economies. . . . The breakdown of the business structure during the war was complete. . . . [R]ehabilitation of the economic structure of Europe quite evidently will require a much longer time and greater effort than had been foreseen. . . .

The truth of the matter is that Europe's requirements for the next 3 or 4 years of foreign food and other essential products—principally from America—are so much greater than her present ability to pay that she must have substantial help or face economic, social, and political deterioration of a very grave character.

The remedy lies in breaking the vicious circle and restoring the confidence of the European people in the economic future of their own countries and of Europe as a whole. . . .

Aside from the demoralizing effect on the world at large and the possibilities of disturbances arising as a result of the desperation of the people concerned, the consequences to the economy of the United States should be apparent to all. It is logical that the United States should do whatever it is able to do to assist in the return of normal economic health in the world, without which there can be no political stability and no assured peace. Our policy is directed not against any country or doctrine but against hunger, poverty, desperation, and chaos. Its purpose should be the revival of a working economy in the world so as to permit the emergence of political and social conditions in which free institutions can exist. Such assistance, I am convinced, must not be on a piecemeal basis as various crises develop. Any assistance that this Government may render in the future should provide a cure rather than a mere palliative. Any government that is willing to assist in the task of recovery will find full cooperation, I am sure, on the part of the United States Government. Any government which maneuvers to block the recovery of other countries cannot expect help from us. Furthermore, governments, political parties, or groups which seek to perpetuate human misery in order to profit therefrom politically or otherwise will encounter the opposition of the United States. . . .

It would be neither fitting nor efficacious for this Government to undertake to draw up unilaterally a program designed to place Europe on its feet economically. This is the business of the Europeans. The initiative, I think, must come from Europe. The role of this country should consist of friendly aid in the drafting of a European program and of later support of such a program so far as it may be practical for us to do so. The program should be a joint one, agreed to by a number, if not all, European nations. . . .

With foresight, and a willingness on the part of our people to face up to the vast responsibility which history has clearly placed upon our country, the difficulties I have outlined can and will be overcome.

The Marshall Plan worked. The European nations recovered, just as economists had predicted they would. A Western effort to rebuild Germany followed. Near the end of World War II, the Allies had agreed to divide Germany into zones. Now the British, French, and Americans merged their zones in an effort to offset the Soviet threat. When the Russians countered by cutting off access to Berlin, which was located within the Soviet zone, the Western powers launched an airlift that succeeded in breaking the blockade. The effort to reconstruct Germany continued.

Next came a military alliance to complement the economic program. The United States took the lead in 1949 in establishing the North Atlantic Treaty Organization (NATO). Twelve nations banded together, vowing that an attack against any one member would be considered an attack against all.

The Soviet Union joined the meeting of European nations to hammer out a request. But the Soviets were suspicious from the start, and instructions to Soviet diplomats told them: "When discussing specific proposals related to American aid to Europe, the Soviet delegation should object to those conditions of this aid that might infringe upon the sovereignty and the economic independence of European nations."

—Instructions for the Soviet delegation to the meeting of foreign ministers in Paris, June 25, 1947

The aid provided by the Marshall Plan helped revive war-torn Europe. Countries such as West Germany welcomed the assistance that would help them avoid communism and maintain their freedom, which this poster calls the "free way," (freie bahn) a play on the German word for highway—"autobahn."

The containment strategy that George Kennan had first recommended in 1946 was now firmly in place. Americans believed that the world faced a fearful threat from communism, which they saw as a contagious disease spreading around the globe. This map, made in 1947 from a United Press survey, showed the geographical distribution of the estimated 20,100,225 Communist Party members scattered throughout the world.

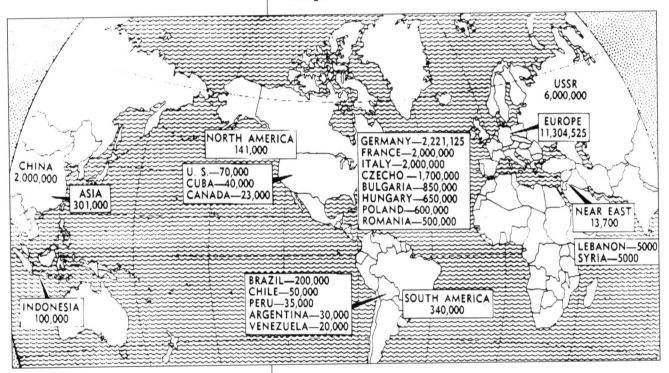

A Soviet Bomb

The framework to contain the cold war came none too soon. In 1949 the United States faced several shocks. One of the most frightening was the discovery that the Soviet Union had developed an atomic bomb. American scientists, working with their British counterparts, had earlier developed the first atomic weapon, at Los Alamos, New Mexico, and the U.S. Air Force had then detonated two devastating bombs, over Hiroshima and Nagasaki in Japan. Some U.S. officials believed that the Russians could not possibly develop their own bomb in less than 15 years. President Truman thought the Soviets might never be able to accomplish such a feat at all. America's scientists, more fully aware of the developmental process,

knew that it could be done far more quickly. Over Labor Day weekend, an air force reconnaissance plane on a routine mission picked up air samples demonstrating higher-than-expected radioactivity counts, revealing that the Russians had tested their first bomb. Truman soon announced the news in a press release.

We have evidence that within recent weeks an atomic explosion occurred in the U.S.S.R.

Ever since atomic energy was first released by man, the eventual development of this new force by other nations was to be expected. This probability has always been taken into account by us.

Nearly 4 years ago I pointed out that "scientific opinion appears to be practically unanimous that the essential theoretical knowledge upon which the discovery is based is already widely known. There is also substantial agreement that foreign research can come abreast of our present theoretical knowledge in time." And, in the Three-Nation Declaration of the president of the United States and the prime ministers of the United Kingdom and Canada, dated November 15, 1945, it was emphasized that no single nation could in fact have a monopoly of atomic weapons.

This recent development emphasizes once again, if indeed such emphasis were needed, the necessity for that truly effective

Top Secret

30 August 1949

This is to report to you that due to the efforts of many Soviet scientists, designers, engineers, managers, and workers of our industry over four years of strenuous work, your assignment to create a Soviet atomic bomb has been fulfilled.

—Report by L. P. Berie and I. V. Kurchatov to I. V. Stalin on preliminary data received during the atomic bomb test

There is only one thing worse than one nation having the atomic bomb—that's two nations having it.

—Physical chemist Harold Urey upon hearing the President's announcement of the end of the U.S. monopoly on atomic weapons

Just as Germany was divided after World War II, the city of Berlin, located within the Soviet sector, was divided as well. When the Soviets shut off land access to West Berlin, which was controlled by the Allies who had fought together in World War II, the United States and Great Britain responded by airlifting supplies into West Berlin. The Tiergarten area pictured here was divided into vegetable gardens to supplement food supplies provided by plane.

enforceable international control of atomic energy which this Government and the large majority of the members of the United Nations support.

The China White Paper

A second shock to the United States came when Mao Zedong and his Communist Party in China triumphed in a long, bitter civil war. Even while China was struggling against Japan in World War II, it had been consumed by conflict between the Nationalists, led by Jiang Jieshi, who wanted to maintain power, and Mao's Communists, who wanted to take over. When Jiang's regime collapsed from internal corruption and external force, he fled to the island of Taiwan, nursing a naive belief that he was still the rightful leader of all China and would someday return to reclaim his place on the mainland.

Americans watched the civil war in China uncomfortably. In August 1949, just months before Mao's ultimate victory, the U. S. government issued a document called "The China White Paper," which outlined the roots of the struggle and offered reasons for the inability of the United States to alter the results. It described how the Kuomintang, the revolutionary organization of Sun Yat-sen and Generalissimo Jiang Jieshi, prevailed for a time but then came under attack by Mao's Chinese communist Party. The civil war was under way as China faced the invasion of the Japanese during World War II.

More than 1,000 pages long, "The China White Paper" aroused the ire of administration opponents, who contended that Truman and his government were not doing enough to stop the communist threat. In his covering letter, Secretary of State Dean Acheson summarized the document for the President.

In accordance with your wish, I have had compiled a record of our relations with China, special emphasis being placed on the last five years. This record is being published and will therefore be available to the Congress and to the people of the United States. . . .

This is a frank record of an extremely complicated and most unhappy period in the life of a great country to which the United States has long been attached by ties of closest friendship. . . .

By the beginning of the twentieth century, the combined force of overpopulation and new ideas set in motion that chain of events

THE SPEAKER'S PLATFORM

Cartoonists seized upon the dramatic events of the cold war and attacked the aggressive initiatives of the Soviet Union. In this drawing, which appeared in 1949, artist Edwin Marcus pictured Soviet leader Joseph Stalin standing on top of a pile of coffins representing nations the Russians had forcibly brought under their control, preaching all the while about American aggression.

Stalin watched carefully what was happening in Asia. Even before World War II ended, he told Chinese Nationalist diplomats that Japan "will restore her might in 20, 30 years. [The] whole plan of our relations with China is based on this."

which can be called the Chinese revolution. It is one of the most imposing revolutions in recorded history and its outcome and consequences are yet to be foreseen. . . .

Representatives of our Government, military and civilian, who were sent to assist the Chinese in prosecuting the war [World War II] soon discovered that . . . the long [revolutionary] struggle had seriously weakened the Chinese Government not only militarily and economically, but also politically and in morale. The reports of United States military and diplomatic officers reveal a growing conviction through 1943 and 1944 that the Government and the Kuomintang had apparently lost the crusading spirit that won the people's loyalty during the early years of the war. In the opinion of many observers they had sunk into corruption, into a scramble for place and power, and into reliance on the United States to win the war for them and to preserve their own domestic supremacy. . . .

It was evident to us that only a rejuvenated and progressive Chinese Government which could recapture the enthusiastic loyalty of the people could and would wage an effective war against Japan. American officials repeatedly brought their concern with this situation to the attention of the Generalissimo and he repeatedly assured them that it would be corrected. He made, however, little or no effective effort to correct it and tended to shut himself off from Chinese officials who gave unpalatable advice. . . .

When peace came the United States was confronted with three possible alternatives in China: (1) it could have pulled out lock, stock and barrel; (2) it could have intervened militarily on a major scale to assist the Nationalists [the governmental forces of Jiang Jieshi] to destroy the Communists; (3) it could, while assisting the Nationalists to assert their authority over as much of China as possible, endeavor to avoid a civil war by working for a compromise between the two sides. . . .

The second objective of assisting the National Government . . . we pursued vigorously from 1945 to 1949. The National Government was the recognized government of a friendly power. Our friendship, and our right under international law alike, called for aid to the Government instead of to the Communists who were seeking to subvert and overthrow it. . . .

The reasons for the failure of the Chinese National Government . . . do not stem from any inadequacy of American aid. . . . The fact was that the decay which our observers had detected . . . early in the war had fatally sapped the powers of resistance of the Kuomintang. Its leaders had proved incapable of meeting the crisis confronting them, its troops had lost the will to

Four Senators—Pat McCarran of Nevada, Styles Bridges of New Hampshire, Kenneth S. Wherry of Nebraska, and William F. Knowland of California—were among those who challenged the arguments of the White Paper. It was, they said, "a 1,054-page whitewash of a wishful, do-nothing policy which has succeeded only in placing Asia in danger of Soviet conquest with its ultimate threat to the peace of the world and our own national security."

During World War II, Chinese communist leader Mao Zedong, shown here with his wife Lan Ping, fought against both the Japanese and the Chinese government of Jiang Jieshi. As Jiang's corruption-riddled regime collapsed and he fled to the island of Taiwan, Mao established his control over the entire Chinese mainland.

While some critics criticized the American government for not stopping the Chinese communists from seizing control, others charged that the United States had behaved as an imperialistic power towards China in the past. This cartoon shows a devious Uncle Sam using the blood of the Chinese people to write a "White Book of U.S. Imperialism."

Twin Cities

Americans often had distorted ideas about China, assuming that this Asian country would behave just like the United States. In 1940, Senator Kenneth S. Wherry of Nebraska described his expectations for one of China's largest cities: "With God's help, we will lift Shanghai up and up, ever up, until it is just like Kansas City."

fight, and its Government had lost popular support. The Communists, on the other hand, through a ruthless discipline and fanatical zeal, attempted to sell themselves as guardians and liberators of the people. The Nationalist armies did not have to be defeated; they disintegrated. History has proved again and again that a regime without faith in itself and an army without morale cannot survive the test of battle. . . .

It has been urged that relatively small amounts of additional aid—military and economic—to the National Government would have enabled it to destroy communism in China. The most trustworthy military, economic, and political information available to our Government does not bear out this view. . . .

The unfortunate but inescapable fact is that the ominous result of the civil war in China was beyond the control of the government of the United States. Nothing that this country did or could have done within the reasonable limits of its capabilities could have changed that result; nothing that was left undone by this country has contributed to it. It was the product of internal Chinese forces, forces which this country tried to influence but could not. A decision was arrived at within China, if only a decision by default. . . .

NSC-68

Troubled by the Soviet bomb and the communist triumph in China, President Truman asked for a full review of the U.S. approach to international affairs. In 1950, the National Security Council, which had been created in 1947 to provide interdepartmental policy coordination, produced a top-secret document known as NSC-68. Written under the direction of Secretary of State Acheson, NSC-68 built upon the Truman Doctrine in describing the challenges facing the United States in cataclysmic terms. It argued that simply proceeding along the course of action already defined was insufficient; the United States needed to take an even more aggressive approach. The document, which was presented to the President in April 1950 though never officially signed, shaped U.S. foreign and defense policy for the next 20 years.

I. Background of the Present World Crisis . . .

Within the past thirty-five years the world has experienced two global wars of tremendous violence. It has witnessed two revolutions—the Russian and the Chinese—of extreme scope and intensity. . . . For several centuries it had proved impossible for any one nation to gain such preponderant strength that a coalition of other nations could not in time face it with greater strength. The international scene was marked by recurring periods of violence and war, but a system of sovereign and independent states was maintained, over which no state was able to achieve hegemony.

Two complex sets of factors have now basically altered this historical distribution of power. First the defeat of Germany and Japan and the decline of the British and French Empires have interacted with the development of the United States and the Soviet Union in such a way that power has increasingly gravitated to these two centers. Second, the Soviet Union, unlike previous aspirants to hegemony, is animated by a new fanatic faith, antithetical to our own, and seeks to impose its absolute authority over the rest of the world. . . .

The issues that face us are momentous, involving the fulfillment or destruction not only of this Republic but of civilization itself. They are issues which will not await our deliberations. With conscience and resolution this Government and the people it represents must now take new and fateful decisions. . . .

As the Chinese communists gained control in Canton, they paraded along the waterfront to celebrate their victory. One of them carried a portrait of Soviet leader Joseph Stalin, whom Mao and his fellow communists admired.

The purpose of NSC-68 was to so bludgeon the mass mind of "top government" that not only could the President make a decision but that the decision could be carried out.

—Secretary of State
Dean Acheson,
in his memoirs

IV. The Underlying Conflict in the Realm of Ideas and Values Between the U.S. Purpose and the Kremlin Design. . . .

The Kremlin regards the United States as the only major threat to the achievement of its fundamental design. There is a basic conflict between the idea of freedom under a government of laws, and the idea of slavery under the grim oligarchy of the Kremlin, which has come to a crisis with the polarization of power. . . and the exclusive possession of atomic weapons by the two protagonists. . . .

Thus unwillingly our free society finds itself mortally challenged by the Soviet system. No other value system is so wholly irreconcilable with ours, so implacable in its purpose to destroy ours, so capable of turning to its own uses the most dangerous and divisive trends in our own society, no other so skillfully and powerfully evokes the elements of irrationality in human nature everywhere, and no other has the support of a great and growing center of military power. . . .

IX. Possible Courses of Action

. . . Four possible courses of action by the United States in the present situation can be distinguished. They are:

a. Continuation of current policies, with current and currently projected programs for carrying out these policies;

b. Isolation;

c. War; and

d. A more rapid building up of the political, economic, and military strength of the free world than provided under A, with the purpose of reaching, if possible, a tolerable state of order among nations without war and of preparing to defend ourselves in the event that the free world is attacked. . . .

A more rapid build-up of political, economic, and military strength and thereby of confidence in the free world than is now contemplated is the only course which is consistent with progress toward achieving our fundamental purpose. . . .

In summary, we must, by means of a rapid and sustained build-up of the political, economic, and military strength of the free world, and by means of an affirmative program intended to wrest the initiative from the Soviet Union, confront it with convincing evidence of the determination and ability of the free world to frustrate the Kremlin design of a world dominated by its will. Such evidence is the only means short of war which eventually may force the Kremlin to abandon its present course of action and to negotiate acceptable agreements on issues of major importance. . . .

War in Korea

Barely two months after the acceptance of NSC-68, the United States found itself facing a major international crisis in Korea. This Asian nation had been partitioned for reasons of military convenience at the very end of World War II. Soviet troops accepted the Japanese surrender north of the 38th parallel of latitude; American troops did the same south of that line. In the next few years, as that temporary line hardened, the Soviet Union set up a government in the north, while the United States established one in the south. The major powers both left Korea but continued to support the regimes they had created. Meanwhile, North Korea and South Korea each sought to reunify the country on its own terms.

On June 25, 1950, North Korean troops invaded South Korea. Surprised, the United States immediately assumed (wrongly, as it turned out) that the attack had been orchestrated by Moscow. President Truman quickly issued a public statement reacting to the assault.

In Korea the Government forces, which were armed to prevent border raids and to preserve internal security, were attacked by invading forces from North Korea. The Security Council of the United Nations called upon the invading troops to cease hostilities

The Korean War was a full-scale military conflict. Although the United Nations authorized the effort to check the North Korean invasion of South Korea, the United States provided most of the manpower and munitions, such as the guns on USS Missouri, which sought to cut North Korean communication lines near the Chinese border.

In my generation, this was not the first occasion when the strong had attacked the weak. . . . I remembered how each time the democracies failed to act it had encouraged the aggressors to keep going ahead. Communism was acting in Korea just as Hitler, Mussolini, and the Japanese had acted ten, fifteen, and twenty years earlier. I felt certain that if South Korea was allowed to fall Communist leaders would be emboldened to override nations closer to our own shores. . . . If this was allowed to go unchallenged it would mean a third world war, just as similar incidents had brought on the second world war.

—President Harry S. Truman, reflecting in his memoirs about his reaction to news about North Korea's attack

and to withdraw to the 38th parallel. This they have not done, but on the contrary have pressed the attack. The Security Council called upon all members of the United Nations to render every assistance to the United Nations in the execution of this resolution. In these circumstances I have ordered United States air and sea forces to give the Korean Government troops cover and support.

The attack upon Korea makes it plain beyond all doubt that communism has passed beyond the use of subversion to conquer independent nations and will now use armed invasion and war. . . .

I know that all members of the United Nations will consider carefully the consequences of this latest aggression in Korea in defiance of the Charter of the United Nations. A return to the rule of force in international affairs would have far-reaching effects. The United States will continue to uphold the rule of law. . . .

First American air and naval forces, then U.S. ground forces, led the way in South Korea. A daring counterattack by United Nations forces under U.S. General Douglas MacArthur that began with a landing at Inchon in September 1950 ended up pushing the North Koreans back across the 38th parallel. This advance fulfilled the initial U.S. aims in the war, but in October MacArthur pressed on, to try to unify Korea on South Korean terms. UN forces moved through North Korea, nearer to the Chinese border. Despite China's signals that it was uncomfortable with this action near its own territory, MacArthur continued his campaign. At the end of November, five months after the war began, the Chinese launched a full-fledged attack that drove UN troops back toward the 38th parallel.

As war turned into stalemate, a bitter conflict developed between MacArthur and Truman. The general wanted to push into North Korea and defeat the enemy, using air strikes and even atomic weapons against the Chinese, but Truman was determined to fight a limited war. He did not want to involve the Soviet Union and weaken U.S. strength elsewhere. He ultimately decided that use of the atomic bomb would be counterproductive. By midwinter 1951 Truman and his military advisors made it clear that they were committed to a limited approach aimed at restoring the pattern that had existed prior to the North Korean attack. U.S. critics attacked Truman's approach. Speaker of the House of Representatives Joseph W. Martin delivered a blistering

General Douglas MacArthur (center, seated) led the American forces in Korea. An able but arrogant military leader, he spearheaded a successful counterattack against the North Koreans but was later relieved of his command when he demanded that the United States fight an even wider war than President Truman intended.

speech challenging the President, then invited MacArthur to respond to the address. In March, the Speaker read MacArthur's inflammatory reply to the entire House.

. . . It seems strangely difficult for some to realize that here in Asia is where the Communist conspirators have elected to make their play for global conquest, and that we have joined the issue thus raised on the battlefield; that here we fight Europe's war with arms while the diplomats there still fight it with words; that if we lose this war to Communism in Asia the fall of Europe is inevitable; win it and Europe most probably would avoid war and yet preserve freedom. As you point out, we must win. There is no substitute for victory.

Truman felt he had no choice but to relieve his insubordinate general; MacArthur had gone too far in criticizing American

Frankly, in the opinion of the Joint Chiefs of Staff, this strategy would involve us in the wrong war, at the wrong place, at the wrong time, and with the wrong enemy.

—General Omar Bradley, Chairman of the U.S. Joint Chiefs of Staff, who did not want the Korean conflict to develop into a war with China

KOREAN WAR
1950–1953

50 km

100 miles

I think the prolonged performance of his one-man act is wearing the patience of the rest of the team mighty thin.

—Congressman Robert Kerr of Oklahoma, responding to MacArthur's statement to the House of Representatives

policy. Worse still, the criticism had been made public and constituted an open challenge to the President himself. Under the U.S. constitutional system, the President is the commander-in-chief and has the final responsibility for making decisions about war and peace. On April 11, 1951, Truman issued the following statement.

With deep regret, I have concluded that General of the Army Douglas MacArthur is unable to give his wholehearted support to the policies of the United States Government and of the United Nations in matters pertaining to his official duties. In view of the specific responsibilities imposed upon me by the Constitution of the United States and the added responsibility which has been entrusted to me by the United Nations, I have decided that I must make a change of command in the Far East. I have, therefore, relieved General MacArthur of his commands and have designated Lieutenant General Matthew B. Ridgeway as his successor.

Full and vigorous debate on matters of national policy is a vital element in the constitutional system of our free democracy. It is fundamental, however, that military commanders must be governed by the policies and directives issued to them in the manner provided by our laws and Constitution. In time of crisis, the consideration is particularly compelling.

Despite the official reprimand, MacArthur returned home to a tumultuous welcome. In a speech before a joint session of the Senate and the House of Representatives, he restated his arguments about policy in Korea and then said farewell.

I am closing my fifty-two years of military service. When I joined the Army even before the turn of the century, it was the fulfillment of all my boyish hopes and dreams. The world has turned over many times since I took the oath on the Plain at West Point, and the hopes and dreams have long since vanished. But I still remember the refrain of one of the most popular barrack ballads of that day which proclaimed most proudly that—

Old soldiers never die, they just fade away.

And like the old soldier of that ballad, I now close my military career and just fade away—an old soldier who tried to do his duty as God gave him the light to see that duty.

Good-by.

Some Americans sympathized with MacArthur because they found the limited aims of the Korean War difficult to understand. Author James A. Michener captured these frustrations in his 1953 novel *The Bridges at Toko-Ri,* the story of U.S. troops on a naval carrier off the Korean coast. Their commander wants to bomb four bridges at a Korean site called Toko-Ri, which he believes will make a major difference in the war. The commander, who lost his sons in World War II, is distressed that Americans at home do not comprehend what is at stake in this struggle. At one point in the novel, Michener describes the admiral worrying about people who seem to ignore the issues being fought over so fiercely in Korea.

He went up on the bridge to check the rolling sea for the last time. "What would they have us abandon to the enemy?" he asked. "Korea? Then Japan and the Philippines? Sooner or later Hawaii?" He walked back and forth pondering this problem of where abandonment would end, and as the sleet howled upon him he could not fix that line: "Maybe California, Colorado. Perhaps we'd stabilize at the Mississippi." He could not say. Instead he held to one unwavering conviction: "A messenger will run in and tell the commissars, 'They even knocked out the bridges at Toko-Ri.' And that's the day they'll quit." Then reason might come into the world.

The Korean War dragged on into Dwight D. Eisenhower's presidency. During the 1952 campaign he promised to go to Korea, and did so three weeks after his election. When truce talks bogged down, his administration privately threatened the use of atomic weapons. Finally, in July 1953, an armistice was signed. The 38th parallel remained the dividing line, but after three long years at least the unpopular war was over.

The war resulted in about 34,000 Americans dead in battle and many more wounded. As many as 2 million Koreans in the North and South may have died, with numerous others injured. The war was also extremely expensive. U.S. defense expenditures soared from $13 billion in 1950 to about $47 billion three years later, along the lines proposed in NSC-68.

The war had important political effects as well. It poisoned relations with the mainland People's Republic of China and prevented the United States from extending formal diplomatic recognition to the new government for more than 20 years.

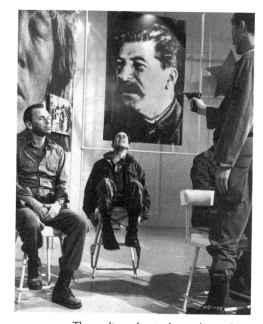

The war lingered on in the popular mind. In 1959, Richard Condon's novel The Manchurian Candidate *appeared, and three years later it became a haunting film. The film showed the capture of an American infantry unit by the North Koreans and pictured the soldiers being brainwashed by a Chinese communist hypnotist. In this still from the film, a hypnotized Raymond Shaw (played by Lawrence Harvey) is killing a fellow soldier sitting under a picture of Soviet leader Joseph Stalin, as another soldier (Frank Sinatra) looks on.*

Choosing Sides

The film version of *The Manchurian Candidate* was clearly a product of the cold war. At one point Raymond's mother (played by Angela Lansbury) declares: "Raymond, if we were at war, and you were suddenly to become infatuated with the daughter of a Russian agent, wouldn't you expect me to come to you and object and beg you to stop the entire thing before it was too late? Well, we are at war. It's a cold war. But it will get worse, and worse, until every man, woman, and child in this country will have to stand up and be counted to say whether they are on the side of right and freedom or on the side of the [traitors] of this country."

Chapter Two

The Anti-communist Crusade

The cold war affected domestic as well as foreign affairs. Fear of the challenges posed by the Soviet Union abroad led to concern that communism was infiltrating American society and threatening the United States. As the nation established its policy of containment in an effort to stop Russian encroachment overseas, it also embarked on a crusade to root out communist influence within American borders wherever evidence of subversion could be found.

All Americans were vulnerable. Those who had dabbled with radical causes during the Great Depression of the 1930s, when the capitalist system seemed to be crumbling, now found themselves under attack. People who had joined the Communist Party briefly during their college years were called upon to explain their actions when young.

At the time the administration of Harry Truman mobilized support for its policy of containing communism around the world, it took the first steps to check the perceived communist threat at home. After being called soft on communism by Republicans who scored substantial gains in the midterm congressional elections of 1946, Truman established a new Federal Employee Loyalty Program in 1947. It ordered the Federal Bureau of Investigation (FBI) to examine its files for evidence of subversive activity and to bring any suspects before a Civil Service Commission Loyalty Review Board. Although the program initially contained safeguards to protect the people being examined, in time an FBI accusation came to be viewed as evidence of guilt.

Meanwhile, Congress embarked on investigations of its own. The House Un-American Activities Committee (HUAC), founded as a special committee in 1938 and then made permanent in 1945, began to

The House Un-American Activities Committee began hearings on the issue of communist subversion in 1947. The hearings often had a circuslike atmosphere, with spectators, photographers, and newsreel camera operators following the questions posed by committee members and the answers of witnesses.

Each person testifying before HUAC had to make a decision about what to do and had to live with the consequences of it for years. Some resisted—and found their careers destroyed by the blacklist. Others, such as movie director Elia Kazan, at first spoke in 1950 about his own Communist Party involvement but refused to name others, then capitulated two years later and named others with whom he had been associated. Some people in the entertainment field never forgave him. Despite such powerful films as his *A Streetcar Named Desire, On the Waterfront, East of Eden,* and *Splendor in the Grass,* the Academy of Motion Picture Arts and Sciences refused to give him a lifetime achievement Honorary Oscar, although it had so honored virtually all of his contemporaries. Not until the March 21, 1999, Academy Awards did Hollywood provide such acknowledgment of his work.

investigate communist infiltration in a series of dramatic hearings after World War II. Its activities, like those of the Truman loyalty program, created a perception that there was a serious problem within the United States and helped legitimize tactics that soon threatened the civil liberties of all U.S. citizens.

Hollywood and HUAC

Hollywood was one of the early targets of congressional investigations. In 1947, HUAC began a probe of the motion picture industry, making the argument that many Hollywood figures had left-wing sympathies that compromised their work. The committee contended that the films they produced had tremendous power to corrupt the American public and therefore threatened the safety and stability of the United States. Pictures sympathetic to the communist menace, HUAC claimed, could undermine American values. In a pattern that developed over the next several years, HUAC issued legal documents known as subpoenas demanding that writers, actors, directors, and producers appear before the committee to divulge how their own political inclinations might have affected their films. Often these well-publicized hearings became heated and contentious. Through them the country became accustomed to the refrain, "Are you now or have you ever been a member of the Communist Party?" The writer Ring Lardner, Jr., was one of those who faced the hostile committee, where he was questioned by chairman J. Parnell Thomas and chief investigator Robert E. Stripling. Lardner wanted to begin by reading a statement, but the committee wanted to find out about the Screen Writers Guild, which it considered subversive.

Mr. LARDNER. Mr. Chairman, I have a short statement I would like to make.

The CHAIRMAN. Have you completed the identification?

Mr. STRIPLING. That is sufficient.

(The witness hands statement to the chairman.). . .

The CHAIRMAN. Mr. Lardner, the committee is unanimous in the fact that after you testify you may read your statement.

Mr. LARDNER. Thank you.

Mr. STRIPLING. Mr. Lardner, you are here before the committee in response to a subpoena served upon you on September 22; is that correct?

Mr. LARDNER. Yes.

Mr. STRIPLING. Mr. Lardner, are you a member of the Screen Writers Guild?

Mr. LARDNER. Mr. Stripling, I want to be cooperative about this, but there are certain limits to my cooperation. I don't want to help you divide or smash this particular guild, or to infiltrate the motion-picture business in any way for the purpose which seems to me to be to try to control that business, to control what the American people can see and hear in their motion-picture theaters.

The CHAIRMAN. Now, Mr. Lardner, don't do like the others, if I were you, or you will never read your statement. I would suggest——

Mr. LARDNER. Mr. Chairman, let me——

The CHAIRMAN. You be responsive to the question.

Mr. LARDNER: I am——

The CHAIRMAN. The question is: Are you a member of the Screen Writers Guild?

Mr. LARDNER. But I understood you to say that I would be permitted to read the statement, Mr. Chairman.

The CHAIRMAN. Yes; after you are finished with the questions and answers——

Mr. LARDNER. Yes. . . .

The CHAIRMAN. All right, then, a congressional committee is asking you: Are you a member of the Screen Writers Guild? Now you answer it "yes" or "no."

Mr. LARDNER. Well, I am saying that in order to answer that——

The CHAIRMAN. All right, put the next question. Go to the $64 question.

The WITNESS. I haven't——

The CHAIRMAN. Go to the next question.

Mr. STRIPLING. Mr. Lardner, are you now or have you ever been a member of the Communist Party?

Mr. LARDNER. Well, I would like to answer that question, too.

As the House Un-American Activities Committee began its investigation of possible communist infiltration of Hollywood, a number of stars—including actors Lauren Bacall and Humphrey Bogart, standing at the bottom of the stairway—came to Washington, D.C., to protest the congressional action.

I'M NO COMMUNIST

The Hollywood stars who came to Washington, D.C., to defend their colleagues who faced the House Un-American Activities Committee found that they, too, were under attack. Humphrey Bogart had to launch a public relations campaign to clear his own name. "Hell, I'm no politician," Bogart declared. "That's what I meant when I said our Washington trip was a mistake."

Mr. STRIPLING. Mr. Lardner, the charge has been made before this committee that the Screen Writers Guild, which, according to the record, you are a member of, whether you admit it or not, has a number of individuals in it who are members of the Communist Party. The committee is seeking to determine the extent of communist infiltration in the Screen Writers Guild and in other guilds within the motion-picture industry.

Mr. LARDNER. Yes.

Mr. STRIPLING. And certainly the question of whether or not you are a member of the Communist Party is very pertinent. Now, are you a member or have you ever been a member of the Communist Party?

Mr. LARDNER. It seems to me you are trying to discredit the Screen Writers Guild through me and the motion-picture industry through the Screen Writers Guild and our whole practice of freedom of expression.

Mr. STRIPLING. If you and others are members of the Communist Party you are the ones who are discrediting the Screen Writers Guild.

Mr. LARDNER. I am trying to answer the question by stating first what I feel about the purpose of the question which, as I say, is to discredit the whole motion-picture industry.

The CHAIRMAN. You won't say anything first. You are refusing to answer this question.

Mr. LARDNER. I am saying my understanding is as an American resident———

The CHAIRMAN. Never mind your understanding. There is a question: Are you or have you ever been a member of the Communist Party?

Mr. LARDNER. I could answer exactly the way you want Mr. Chairman———

The CHAIRMAN. No———

Mr. LARDNER (continuing). But I think that is a———

The CHAIRMAN. It is not a question of our wanting you to answer that. It is a very simple question. Anybody would be proud to answer it—any real American would be proud to answer the question, "Are you now or have you ever been a member of the Communist Party"—any real American.

Mr. LARDNER. It depends on the circumstances. I could answer it, but if I did I would hate myself in the morning.

The CHAIRMAN. Leave the witness chair.

Mr. LARDNER. It was a question that would———

The CHAIRMAN. Leave the witness chair.

Mr. LARDNER. Because it is a question——
The CHAIRMAN (pounding gavel). Leave the witness chair.
Mr. LARDNER. I think I am leaving by force.
The CHAIRMAN. Sergeant, take the witness away.
(Applause.)

Altogether, HUAC called 19 Hollywood figures to testify. Ten of the accused, including Lardner and fellow writer Dalton Trumbo, refused to answer the question whether or not they were or had been members of the Communist Party, by invoking their constitutional right to remain silent. The committee responded by threatening prison terms if they failed to testify, but they held their ground. When the committee refused to budge, they went to prison for contempt of Congress and served sentences ranging from six months to one year.

At that point, Hollywood capitulated totally. On the day Congress voted the contempt citations, 50 motion-picture executives held a meeting at the Waldorf-Astoria Hotel in New York at which they condemned the so-called Hollywood Ten and took harsh measures to head off further attacks from the committee. The executives issued a statement that summed up their capitulation. It introduced the "blacklist,"

As Hollywood caved in to the House Un-American Activities Committee, filmmakers also made a number of aggressively anticommunist films, such as The Red Menace of 1949, to demonstrate their own loyalty and patriotism.

Many branches of the entertainment industry capitulated to the anticommunist attack. Red Channels, a booklet published in New York in 1950, listed the compromising left-wing activities of a number of major radio and television personalities, such as actor Jose Ferrer and writer Dashiell Hammett.

whereby any Hollywood actor, writer, or director suspected of radical sympathies was unable to get a job.

Members of the Association of Motion Picture Producers deplore the action of the ten Hollywood men who had been cited for contempt. We do not desire to prejudge their legal rights, but their actions have been a disservice to their employers and have impaired their usefulness to the industry.

We will forthwith discharge or suspend without compensation those in our employ and we will not re-employ any of the ten until such time as he is acquitted or has purged himself of contempt and declares under oath that he is not a Communist.

On the broader issues of alleged subversive and disloyal elements in Hollywood, our members are likewise prepared to take positive action.

We will not knowingly employ a Communist nor a member of any party or groups which advocates the overthrow of the Government of the United States by force or by illegal or unconstitutional methods. In pursuing this policy, we are not going to be swayed by hysteria or intimidation from any source. We are frank to recognize that such a policy involves dangers and risks. There is the danger of hurting innocent people. There is the risk of creating an atmosphere of fear. Creative work at its best cannot be carried on in an atmosphere of fear. We will guard against this danger, this risk, this fear. To this end we will invite the Hollywood talent guilds to work with us to eliminate any subversives, to protect the innocent, and to safeguard free speech and a free screen wherever threatened.

Chambers vs. Hiss

At the same time that HUAC was investigating Hollywood, the committee became involved in another highly visible case, against Alger Hiss, a distinguished member of Franklin D. Roosevelt's administration. In 1948, Whittaker Chambers, a successful *Time* magazine editor who had been a member of the Communist Party, accused Hiss of having been a communist too. Hiss, who had served during both FDR's New Deal and World War II, was highly respected. If he had communist ties, as Chambers charged, then it seemed possible that the entire U.S. government might be tainted. As he was interrogated by chief investigator Stripling and Representatives

Karl E. Mundt, John E. Rankin, and John McDowell, Chambers made his accusations clear.

Mr. STRIPLING. Will you state your full name?

Mr. CHAMBERS. My name is David Whittaker Chambers. . . .

Mr. STRIPLING. What is your present occupation?

Mr. CHAMBERS. I am senior editor of *Time* magazine. . . .

Mr. STRIPLING. When did you first join the Communist Party?

Mr. CHAMBERS. 1924. . . .

Mr. STRIPLING. How long did you remain a member of the Communist Party?

Mr. CHAMBERS. Until 1937. . . .

Mr. STRIPLING. Mr. Chambers, in your statement you stated that you yourself had served the underground, chiefly in Washington, D.C. What underground apparatus are you speaking of and when was it established?

Mr. CHAMBERS. Perhaps we should make a distinction at the beginning. It is Communist theory and practice that even in countries where the Communist Party is legal, an underground party exists side by side with the open party.

The apparatus in Washington was an organization or group of that underground.

Mr. RANKIN. When you speak of the apparatus in Washington you mean the Communist cell, do you not?

Mr. CHAMBERS. I mean in effect a group of Communist cells. . . .

Mr. STRIPLING. Who comprised this cell or apparatus to which you referred?

Mr. CHAMBERS. The apparatus was organized with a leading group of seven men, each of whom was a leader of the cell.

Mr. STRIPLING. Could you name the seven individuals?

Mr. CHAMBERS. The head of the group as I have said was at first Nathan Witt. Other members of the group were Lee Pressman, Alger Hiss, Donald Hiss, Victor Perlo, Charles Kramer——

Mr. STRIPLING. Do you know where in the Government these seven individuals were employed?

Mr. CHAMBERS. I did at one time. I think I could remember some of them. . . .

Mr. STRIPLING. I have here the employment record of Alger Hiss.

For the Record

Newspapers and radio broadcasts carried the story of Whittaker Chambers's testimony against Alger Hiss, and Hiss responded immediately by sending a telegram to the committee:

"My attention has been called by representatives of the press to statements made about me before your committee this morning by one Whittaker Chambers. I do not know Mr. Chambers and, so far as I am aware, have never laid eyes on him. There is no basis for the statements about me made to your committee. I would appreciate it if you would make this telegram a part of your committee's records and I would further appreciate the opportunity of appearing before your committee to make these statements formally and under oath. . . ."

Mr. MUNDT. I think you should read that into the record, including his present employment.

Mr. STRIPLING. [From] 1929 to 1930 he was secretary and law clerk to a Supreme Court justice. From 1930 until 1933 he was engaged in the practice of law.

Mr. RANKIN. May I ask what Supreme Court justice was he clerk for?

Mr. STRIPLING. I will furnish that for you, Mr. Rankin. [It was Oliver Wendell Holmes.]. . . From 1933 to 1935 he was employed by the Agricultural Adjustment Administration. However, during the year 1934 he was also attached to a special Senate committee investigating the munitions industry.

In 1935 he was employed as a special attorney by the Department of Justice. September 13, 1936, he was appointed an assistant to the Assistant Secretary of State. That is the information that I have as of this time. . . .

Mr. STRIPLING. When you left the Communist Party in 1937 did you approach any of these seven to break with you?

Mr. CHAMBERS. No. The only one of those people whom I approached was Alger Hiss. I went to the Hiss home one evening at what I considered considerable risk to myself and found Mrs. Hiss at home. Mrs. Hiss is also a member of the Communist Party.

Mr. MUNDT. Mrs. Alger Hiss?

Mr. CHAMBERS. Mrs. Alger Hiss. Mrs. Donald Hiss, I believe, is not.

Mrs. Hiss attempted while I was there to make a call, which I can only presume was to other Communists, but I quickly went to the telephone and she hung up, and Mr. Hiss came in shortly afterward, and we talked and I tried to break him away from the party.

As a matter of fact, he cried when we separated, when I left him, but he absolutely refused to break.

Mr. McDOWELL. He cried?

Mr. CHAMBERS. Yes, he did. I was very fond of Mr. Hiss.

Mr. MUNDT. He must have given you some reason why he did not want to sever the relationship.

Mr. CHAMBERS. His reasons were simply the party line.

Two days later, on August 5, Hiss testified before the Committee on Un-American Activities. Denying that he had ever met Chambers, Hiss steadfastly disavowed the charges against himself, proclaimed his innocence, and impressed the committee with his straightforward approach. Yet discrepancies between his testimony and that of Chambers

Congressman Richard Nixon was a member of the Committee on Un-American Activities. After Hiss testified, Nixon reflected on the impression Hiss had made on him: "It was a virtuoso performance. Without actually saying it, he left the clear impression that he was the innocent victim of a terrible case of mistaken identity, or that a fantastic vendetta had been launched against him for some reason he could not fathom."

were troubling to some committee members, and the main interrogators—chief investigator Stripling and Representatives Mundt, Rankin, and McDowell—were determined to see if they could uncover the truth.

Mr. HISS. Mr. Chairman, may I be permitted to make a brief statement to the committee?. . .

I am here at my own request to deny unqualifiedly various statements about me which were made before this committee by one Whittaker Chambers the day before yesterday. I appreciate the committee's having promptly granted my request. I welcome the opportunity to answer to the best of my ability any inquiries the members of this committee may wish to ask me.

I am not and never have been a member of the Communist Party. I do not and never have adhered to the tenets of the Communist Party. I am not and never have been a member of any Communist-front organization. I have never followed the Communist Party line, directly or indirectly. To the best of my knowledge, none of my friends is a Communist.

As a State Department official, I have had contacts with representatives of foreign governments, some of whom have

At a Presidential press conference after Hiss testified, a reporter asked Harry Truman, "Mr. President, do you think that the Capitol Hill spy scare is a red herring to divert the public attention from inflation?" Truman agreed that it was.

The long-awaited face-to-face meeting between Whittaker Chambers and Alger Hiss generated newspaper headlines and left people wondering who was telling the truth. The spectator reading the paper seems unaware that he was sitting next to Chambers himself.

Alger Hiss, accompanied here by his wife Priscilla, steadfastly asserted his own innocence throughout all the hearings and trials. Nonetheless, in 1950 a jury found him guilty of two counts of perjury, and Hiss served a four-year sentence.

For many Americans, the Hiss case seemed to prove that there was a real communist threat in the United States. As Richard Nixon observed, "The Hiss case, for the first time, forcibly demonstrated to the American people that domestic communism was a real and present danger to the security of the nation."

undoubtedly been members of the Communist Party, as, for example, representatives of the Soviet Government. My contacts with any foreign representative who could possibly have been a Communist have been strictly official.

To the best of my knowledge, I never heard of Whittaker Chambers until in 1947, when two representatives of the Federal Bureau of Investigation asked me if I knew him and various other people, some of whom I knew and some of whom I did not know. I said I did not know Chambers. So far as I know, I have never laid eyes on him, and I should like to have the opportunity to do so. . . .

Mr. MUNDT. I want to say for one member of the committee that it is extremely puzzling that a man who is senior editor of *Time* magazine, by the name of Whittaker Chambers, whom I had never seen until a day or two ago, and whom you say you have never seen——

Mr. HISS. As far as I know, I have never seen him.

Mr. MUNDT. . . . Should come before this committee and discuss the Communist apparatus working in Washington, which he says is transmitting secrets to the Russian Government, and he lists a group of seven people—Nathan Witt, Lee Pressman, Victor

Donald Hiss——

Mr. HISS. That is eight.

Mr. MUNDT. There seems to be no question about the subversive connections of the six other than the Hiss brothers, and I wonder what possible motive a man who edits *Time* magazine would have for mentioning Donald Hiss and Alger Hiss in connection with those other six.

Mr. HISS. So do I, Mr. Chairman. I have no possible understanding of what could have motivated him. There are many possible motives, I assume, but I am unable to understand it.

Mr. MUNDT. You can appreciate the position of this committee when the name bobs up in connection with those associations.

Mr. HISS. I hope the committee can appreciate my position, too.

Mr. MUNDT. We surely can and that is why we responded with alacrity to your request to be heard.

Mr. HISS. I appreciate that.

Mr. MUNDT. All we are trying to do is find the facts.

Mr. HISS. I wish I could have seen Mr. Chambers before he testified. . . .

Mr. STRIPLING. You say you have never seen Mr. Chambers?

Mr. HISS. The name means absolutely nothing to me, Mr. Stripling.

Mr. STRIPLING. I have here, Mr. Chairman, a picture which was made last Monday by the Associated Press. I understand from people who knew Mr. Chambers during 1934 and '35 that he is much heavier today than he was at that time, but I show you this picture, Mr. Hiss, and ask you if you have ever known an individual who resembles this picture.

Mr. HISS. I would much rather see the individual. I have looked at all the pictures I was able to get hold of in, I think it was, yesterday's paper which had the pictures. If this is a picture of Mr. Chambers, he is not particularly unusual looking. He looks like a lot of people. I might even mistake him for the chairman of this committee. [Laughter.]. . .

Mr. STRIPLING. Mr. Chairman, there is a very sharp contradiction here in the testimony. I certainly suggest Mr. Chambers be brought back before the committee and clear this up. . . .

Mr. MUNDT. The Chair wishes to express the appreciation of the committee for your very cooperative attitude, for your forthright statements, and for the fact that you were first among those whose names were mentioned by various witnesses to communicate

Incriminating Evidence

Richard Nixon was suspicious of Hiss and kept the case alive. In late 1948, Chambers broadened his charge to assert that Hiss was a spy, and took investigators to Chambers's farm in Maryland, where he produced a number of rolls of microfilm that had been hidden in a scooped-out pumpkin. Some of the documents on microfilm were State Department papers typed on a machine Hiss had once owned.

With this evidence, Hiss was indicted for perjury—lying under oath about his involvement with the communists—because the statute of limitations for issuing an indictment for espionage had run out some years before. The first trial ended in a hung jury, lacking the unanimity needed for a conviction. A second trial, in January 1950, convicted Hiss and sent him to jail for four years.

The recently-declassified Venona Project reveals an American spy operation during World War II that decoded Soviet intelligence traffic and shows the extensive assistance provided by the American Communist Party (CPUSA) to the Soviet espionage effort. One cable from November 1944 had a reference to Ethel Rosenberg. In the following passage, in which Liberal is the code name for Julius, Soviet intelligence noted that Ethel knew what her husband was doing: "Information on Liberal's wife. Surname that of her husband, first name Ethel, 29 years old. Married five years. Finished secondary school. A Fellow-countryman [member of the CPUSA] since 1938. Sufficiently well developed politically. Knows about her husband's work and the role of Meter [another agent] and Nil [unidentified agent]. In view of delicate health does not work. Is characterized positively and as a devoted person."

The Rosenbergs had been prepared for Julius's sentence, but the death sentence for Ethel took them by surprise. Locked in separate but nearby cells in the basement of the courthouse as they waited to be taken back to prison, each tried to bolster the spirits of the other. Ethel sang the aria of love and longing "Un bel dì" from the opera *Madama Butterfly*. Julius responded by singing "The Battle Hymn of the Republic."

with us asking for an opportunity to deny the charges.

Mr. RANKIN. And another thing. I want to congratulate the witness that he didn't refuse to answer the questions on the ground that it might incriminate him, and he didn't bring a lawyer here to tell him what to say. . . .

The Rosenbergs on Trial

Later, in the summer of 1950, another case rocked the nation. Federal officials arrested Julius and Ethel Rosenberg, a young New York City couple with radical political sympathies, for allegedly passing atomic secrets to the Soviet Union during World War II. Liberals claimed that the Rosenbergs were innocent victims of cold war hysteria. Conservatives charged that they were further examples of subversion that was threatening the very survival of the United States.

Testimony by Ethel's brother, an employee in the Manhattan Project to create the first atomic bomb, revealed that he had shared top-secret material with Julius, which was then passed on to the Russians. Though Ethel was not involved in the espionage, the government prosecuted her as well in an effort to force Julius to admit his guilt. Neither capitulated, even when they were found guilty in federal court.

When the Rosenbergs returned to court for sentencing on April 5, 1951, they faced Judge Irving Kaufman, who made an impassioned statement blaming U.S. servicemen's deaths in the Korean War on their treachery. This address to the Rosenbergs reflected vividly the anticommunist hysteria of the time.

Because of the seriousness of this case and the lack of precedence, I have refrained from asking the Government for a recommendation. The responsibility is so great that I believe that the Court alone should assume this responsibility.

In view of the importance of the sentences I am about to impose, I believe it is my duty to give some explanation respecting them. . . .

Espionage, as viewed here today, does not reflect the courage of a Nathan Hale [a Revolutionary War spy], risking his life in the service of his own country. It is rather a sordid, dirty work—however idealistic are the rationalizations of the persons who engaged

Julius and Ethel Rosenberg insisted that they were innocent of atomic espionage, but in 1951 a court found them guilty of having passed secrets to the Soviet Union. After the verdict was announced, they were transported back to prison in a patrol car.

in it,—with but one paramount theme, the betrayal of one's own country.

Citizens of this country who betray their fellow-countrymen can be under none of the delusions about the benignity of Soviet power that they might have been prior to World War II. The nature of Russian terrorism is now self-evident. Idealism as a rationale dissolves.

The issue of punishment in this case is presented in a unique framework of history. It is so difficult to make people realize that this country is engaged in a life and death struggle with a completely different system. This struggle is not only manifested externally between these two forces but this case indicates quite clearly that it also involves the employment by the enemy of secret as well as overt outspoken forces among our own people. All of our democratic institutions are, therefore, directly involved in this great conflict. I believe that never at any time in our history were we ever confronted to the same degree that we are today with such a challenge to our very existence. The atom bomb was unknown when the espionage statute was drafted. I emphasize this because we must realize that we are dealing with a missile of destruction which can wipe out millions of Americans.

The competitive advantage held by the United States in super-weapons has put a premium on the services of a new school of spies—the homegrown variety that places allegiance to a foreign power before loyalty to the United States. The punishment to be meted out in this case must therefore serve the maximum interest for the preservation of our society against these traitors in our midst. . . .

What I am about to say is not easy for me. . . . I am convinced, however, that I would violate the solemn and sacred trust that the people of this land have placed in my hands were I to show leniency to the defendants Rosenberg.

I consider your crime worse than murder. Plain deliberate contemplated murder is dwarfed in magnitude by comparison with the crime you have committed. In committing the act of murder, the criminal kills only his victim. The immediate family is brought to grief and when justice is meted out the chapter is closed. But in your case, I believe your conduct in putting into the hands of the Russians the A-bomb years before our best scientists predicted Russia would perfect the bomb has already caused, in my opinion, the Communist aggression in Korea, with the resultant casualties exceeding 50,000 and who knows but that millions more of innocent people may pay the price of your treason. Indeed, by your betrayal you undoubtedly have altered the course of history to the disadvantage of our country. No one can say that we do not live in a constant state of tension. We have evidence of your treachery all around us every day—for the civilian defense activities throughout the nation are aimed at preparing us for an atom bomb attack. . . .

It is not in my power, Julius and Ethel Rosenberg, to forgive you. Only the Lord can find mercy for what you have done.

The sentence of the Court upon Julius and Ethel Rosenberg is, for the crime for which you have been convicted, you are hereby sentenced to the punishment of death, and it is ordered upon some day within the week beginning with Monday, May 21st, you shall be executed according to law.

After the imposition of the Rosenbergs' sentences, the case wound its way through the appeals process. The death sentences were upheld by the U.S. Circuit Court of Appeals on February 25, 1952. As the execution date came closer, the case attracted worldwide attention, with some people pleading for the Rosenbergs' lives and others demanding their deaths. Supporters of the Rosenbergs argued that it would be wrong to leave their two sons orphans. Opponents replied that they were unfit parents whose boys would be better off in another family. Julius and Ethel communicated

Americans who believed that the Rosenbergs were guilty demonstrated in favor of the death penalty. Their signs reflected the depth of their anticommunist sentiment.

Some Americans argued that the Rosenbergs were scapegoats who were being punished for their radical political beliefs. As the time approached for the execution of the Rosenbergs in the electric chair, a throng in New York City asserted their innocence.

with each other during this harrowing time by writing letters describing the politics of the case, their fears for the impact of the case on their young children, and their affection for each other. The next year, after all requests for clemency were turned down, both Julius and Ethel Rosenberg were executed in the electric chair on June 19, 1953.

The day after the appeals court decision, Ethel wrote in a letter to Julius:

My dear one,

Last night at 10:00 o'clock, I heard the shocking news. At the present moment, with little or no detail to hand, it is difficult for me to make any comment, beyond an expression of horror at the shameless haste with which the government appears to be pressing for our liquidation. Certainly, it proves that all our contributions in the past regarding the political nature of our case, have been amazingly correct.

My heart aches for the children, unfortunately they are old enough to have heard for themselves, and no matter what amount of control I am able to exercise, my brain reels, picturing their terror. . . .

Sweetheart, if only I could truly comfort you, I love you so very dearly. . . .

As execution became imminent, Julius wrote to Ethel:

Ethel Darling,

What does one write to his beloved when faced with the very grim reality that in eighteen days, on their 14th wedding anniversary, it is ordered that they be put to death? The approaching darkest hour of our trial and the grave peril that threatened us require every effort on our part to avoid hysteria and false heroics, but only maintain a sober and calm approach to our most crucial problems. . . .

Dearest, over and over again, I have tried to analyze in the most objective manner possible the answers to the position of our government in our case. Everything indicates only one answer—that the wishes of certain madmen are being followed in order to use this case as a coercive bludgeon against all dissenters. However, I still have faith that the more responsible elements in the administration will let sanity be the better part of judgment and save our lives. It seems to me that at this moment it is still touch and go, and therefore we must see to it that the maximum is done in our behalf. . . .

All the love I possess is yours——

Senator Joe McCarthy

As the Rosenberg case unfolded, the anticommunist movement was further galvanized by the actions of Senator Joseph R. McCarthy. On February 9, 1950, not long after the conviction of Alger Hiss, the junior senator from Wisconsin addressed the Women's Republican Club of Wheeling, West Virginia. Searching for an issue as he contemplated a re-election campaign in two years, he seized on the issue of communists in government, which was gaining tremendous attention in the press. In his Lincoln Day speech, McCarthy claimed to have in his hand a list with the names of 205 known communists in the State Department. When pressed

for details, he replied that he would release the list only to the President of the United States. Suddenly finding himself the focus of intense public attention, he realized that he had no copy of the speech he had given. A week and a half later, he inserted a reconstruction of that speech into the _Congressional Record_, declaring in this version that he had a list of 57 subversives. Thus began a vicious mudslinging campaign that consumed the United States for the next four years.

Five years after a world war has been won, men's hearts should anticipate a long peace, and men's minds should be free from the heavy weight that comes with war. But this is not such a period—for this is not a period of peace. This is a time of the "cold war." This is a time when all the world is split into two vast, increasingly hostile armed camps—a time of a great armaments race. . . .

Today we are engaged in a final, all-out battle between communistic atheism and Christianity. The modern champions of communism have selected this as the time. And, ladies and gentlemen, the chips are down—they are truly down. . . .

Ladies, and gentlemen, can there be anyone here tonight who is so blind as to say that the war is not on? Can there be anyone who fails to realize that the Communist world has said, "The time is now"—that this is the time for the show-down between the democratic Christian world and the Communist atheist world?

Unless we face this fact, we shall pay the price that must be paid by those who wait too long.

Six years ago, at the time of the first conference to map out the peace . . . there was within the Soviet orbit 180,000,000 people. Lined up on the antitotalitarian side there were in the world at that time roughly 1,625,000,000 people. Today, only 6 years later, there are 800,000,000 people under the absolute domination of Soviet Russia—an increase of over 400 percent. On our side, the figure has shrunk to around 500,000,000. In other words, in less than 6 years the odds have changed from 9 to 1 in our favor to 8 to 5 against us. This indicates the swiftness of the tempo of Communist victories and American defeats in the cold war. . . .

The reason why we find ourselves in a position of impotency is not because our only powerful potential enemy has sent men to invade our shores, but rather because of the traitorous actions of those who have been treated so well by this Nation. It has not been the less fortunate or members of minority groups who have been selling this Nation out, but rather those who have had all the benefits that the wealthiest nation on earth has had to offer—the

On the Warpath

After his speech in West Virginia on communists in government, McCarthy returned to Washington to amplify his accusations on the floor of the Senate. Early reactions to him were negative. Richard Nixon and other members of the House Un-American Activities Committee thought he was a disaster. Senator Robert A. Taft, a leading Republican, said of McCarthy's Senate speech, "It was a perfectly reckless performance." When, a few weeks later, however, Taft realized the political advantages of what McCarthy was doing, he changed his approach, saying, "If one case doesn't work, try another."

finest homes, the finest college education, and the finest jobs in Government we can give.

This is glaringly true in the State Department. There the bright young men who are born with silver spoons in their mouths are the ones who have been worst. . . .

In my opinion the State Department, which is one of the most important government departments, is thoroughly infested with Communists.

I have in my hand 57 cases of individuals who would appear to be either card carrying members or certainly loyal to the Communist Party, but who nevertheless are still helping to shape our foreign policy.

One thing to remember in discussing the Communists in our Government is that we are not dealing with spies who get 30 pieces of silver to steal the blueprints of a new weapon. We are dealing with a far more sinister type of activity because it permits the enemy to guide and shape our policy. . . .

McCarthy was a demagogue who delighted in playing upon his often disheveled, unshaven, half-sober appearance. He used obscenity freely as he lashed out at his enemies and promoted his own cause. He used maps to show the insidious spread of communism. And he played fast and loose with facts.

McCarthy took on assorted targets, including George C. Marshall, who was the architect of victory in World War II and the creator of the Marshall Plan to rebuild Europe after the war, a man of unimpeachable character. When Republicans gained control of the Senate in the election of 1952, McCarthy's power grew. He became chairman of the Government Operations Committee and head of its Permanent Investigations Subcommittee. He relied on two dedicated assistants, Roy M. Cohn and G. David Schine, to keep attention focused on the alleged communist threat.

McCarthy had public opinion on his side during these years. The Gallup Poll revealed considerable popular support. One poll, on May 21, 1950, asked respondents whether they had been following the news about McCarthy.

In taking on George Marshall, McCarthy claimed that the general was part of "a conspiracy so immense and an infamy so black as to dwarf any previous such venture in the history of man."

Have you heard or read anything about Senator Joseph McCarthy's charges that there are Communists in the State Department in Washington?

COMMUNIST PARTY ORGANIZATION U.S.A.-FEB. 9, 1950

Senator Joseph R. McCarthy was one of the most vocal anticommunists in the United States. He argued that communist infiltration was spreading rapidly and threatening American stability and had to be resisted wherever it appeared.

Yes 84%
No 16%

The same poll then continued by asking those who responded in the affirmative, "Some people say these charges are doing the country more harm than good. What do you, yourself, think—are Senator McCarthy's charges doing harm to the country or are they a good thing for the country?"

Harm 29%
Good 39%
No opinion. 16%
No response. 16%

Another poll, on January 16, 1953, showed that most people knew who McCarthy was, and that many continued to approve of what he was doing. Respondents were asked, "Can you identify Joseph McCarthy?"

Correct. 80%
Incorrect, don't know 20%

The poll continued by asking of those who could identify Senator McCarthy, "In general do you approve or disapprove of the methods used by Senator McCarthy?"

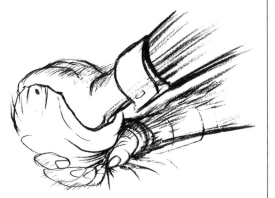

In the 1950s, as McCarthy attacked anyone he deemed subversive, some Americans began to worry about the threat to democratic values. This drawing by cartoonist Robert Osborn— titled "Silence dissenters!"—expressed the view that the anticommunist campaign threatened the right to free speech.

As *The Crucible* played on Broadway, many critics interpreted it as a parable of McCarthyism. David Alman, a novelist and playwright who helped organize the National Committee to Secure Justice in the Rosenberg Case, felt it was "really about the Rosenbergs."

Approve	38%
Disapprove	47%
No opinion	5%

Cultural Responses

The fear of communism permeated American culture. Innocent people found themselves attacked and then denied the right to defend themselves. Some critics protested the vicious charges. Simply being questioned was sometimes taken as a sign of guilt. Americans sympathetic to radical causes had the most difficulty of all. W.E.B. DuBois, the 83-year-old black intellectual and civil rights advocate, was arrested in 1950 for being a member of an organization that sought world peace, including peace with the Soviet Union, and was denied a passport that would have allowed him to travel abroad. Noted black actor and singer Paul Robeson, who was a powerful advocate for black equality and protested the racist patterns of American society, likewise lost his passport and saw his career ruined.

The most vivid protests came on the stage and on the screen. In 1952, Arthur Miller's play *The Crucible* was a thinly veiled attack on the anticommunist crusade. It described the hysteria that descended on Salem, Massachusetts, in 1692 when a group of young women accused other members of the community of being witches and some of the victims were put to death. In his description at the beginning of the script, Miller wrote of the "coming madness" and the "panic" that consumed Salem. Then he told the story of John Proctor, a married man who finds himself accused of witchcraft by his rejected lover. At first Proctor is willing to acknowledge his own involvement with the Devil to save his own life, but he balks when asked by Deputy Governor Danforth and the prosecution to identify others:

PROCTOR: I speak my own sins; I cannot judge another. (*Crying out, with hatred*): I have no tongue for it. . . .

DANFORTH (*considers; then with dissatisfaction*): Come, then, sign your testimony. . . . Come, man, sign it.

PROCTOR (*after glancing at the confession*): You have all witnessed it—it is enough.

DANFORTH: You will not sign it?

PROCTOR: You have all witnessed it; what more is needed?

When the prosecution persists, arguing that the village must have proof, Proctor responds:

> PROCTOR: Damn the village! I confess to God, and God has seen my name on this! It is enough.
> DANFORTH: No, sir, it is——
> PROCTOR: You came to save my soul, did you not? Here! I have confessed myself; it is enough!

Danforth becomes increasingly frustrated.

> DANFORTH: Then explain to me, Mr. Proctor, why you will not let——
> PROCTOR (*with a cry of his whole soul*): Because it is my name! Because I cannot have another in my life! Because I lie and sign myself to lies! Because I am not worth the dust on the feet of them that hang! How may I live without my name? I have given you my soul; leave me my name!

High Noon, a popular film starring Gary Cooper and Grace Kelly, which also appeared in 1952, likewise captured the mood of the time. It told the story of a western town where marshal Will Kane is about to leave his post after marrying a beautiful Quaker woman named Amy Fowler. Five years earlier, Kane had sent Frank Miller, an outlaw, to the penitentiary for murder and driven his gang away. Now, on the day of his wedding, word comes that the sentence has been commuted, the inmate has been freed, and the outlaw gang is on its way back to town to avenge the marshal's deed. The train is due at noon, in about an hour's time. Amy wants Will to leave town with her, but he feels that someone needs to stand up to the outlaw gang or no one in town will ever be safe again. Kane—reflecting on why he needs to stand up to the outlaws, even if no one else will help him—represents the effort to stop McCarthy before it is too late.

It's no good. I've got to go back, Amy.

When Amy protests, he responds that he needs to stay:

I've got to. That's the whole thing. . . . He'll just come after us. . . . They'd come after us and we'd have to run again, as long as we lived.

The film High Noon *was a Western that dramatized the need to stand up to outlaws on the rampage. At the same time, it suggested the need to resist the wild anticommunist efforts of Joseph McCarthy before they poisoned the political climate in the United States.*

Amy tells him not to be a hero as she makes up her own mind to leave alone, and Will responds:

If you think I like this, you're crazy.

Army vs. McCarthy

As the witch hunt continued, McCarthy finally went too far. When the army drafted his assistant David Schine and refused to allow the preferential treatment demanded by his subcommittee's chief counsel Roy Cohn, McCarthy decided to investigate the army itself for subversion.

The Army–McCarthy hearings began in April 1954 and lasted for 36 days. They were televised nationwide, allowing millions of viewers finally to see McCarthy at first hand. They were troubled by the savage attacks he made and became disturbed as they learned how he fabricated evidence with little regard for the facts. As the hearings dragged on, people proved less inclined to give McCarthy their support. The climactic moment in the hearings came when the army's attorney, Boston lawyer Joseph Welch of the Hale & Dorr firm, challenged McCarthy himself.

When McCarthy brought up the left-wing associations of Fred Fisher, one of Welch's own assistants, in direct violation of an agreement with Cohn to keep Fisher's name out of the hearings, Welch was furious. In this session, chaired by Senator Karl Mundt, Welch counterattacked with his own quiet eloquence.

As the Army–McCarthy hearings continued, Americans who had been sympathetic to McCarthy's efforts in the past began to change their minds. Gallup Polls showed the erosion of support for McCarthy.

Mr. WELCH. Mr. Chairman, under these circumstances I must have something approaching a personal privilege.

Senator MUNDT. You may have it, sir. It will not be taken out of your time.

1954	% Favorable	% Unfavorable	No Opinion
January	50	29	21
March	46	36	18
April	38	46	16
May	35	49	16
June	34	45	21

Mr. WELCH. Senator McCarthy, I did not know——Senator, sometimes you say "May I have your attention?"

Senator McCARTHY. I am listening to you. I can listen with one ear.

Mr. WELCH. This time I want you to listen with both.

Senator McCARTHY. Yes

Mr. WELCH. Senator McCarthy, I think until this moment——

Senator McCARTHY. Jim, will you get the news story to the effect that this man belonged to this Communist-front organization? Will you get the citations showing that this was the legal arm of the Communist Party, and the length of time that he belonged, and the fact that he was recommended by Mr. Welch? I think that should be in the record.

Mr. WELCH. You won't need anything in the record when I have finished telling you this.

Until this moment, Senator, I think I never really gauged your cruelty or your recklessness. Fred Fisher is a young man who went to the Harvard Law School and came into my firm and is starting what looks to be a brilliant career with us.

When I decided to work for this committee I asked Jim St. Clair, who sits on my right, to be my first assistant. I said to Jim, "Pick somebody in the firm who works under you that you would like." He chose Fred Fisher and they came down on an afternoon plane. That night, when he had taken a little stab at trying to see what the case was about, Fred Fisher and Jim St. Clair and I went to dinner together. I then said to these two young men, "Boys, I don't know anything about you except I have always liked you, but if there is anything funny in the life of either one of you that would hurt anybody in this case you speak up quick."

Fred Fisher said, "Mr. Welch, when I was in law school, and for a period of months after, I belonged to the Lawyers Guild," as you have suggested, Senator. He went on to say, "I am secretary of the Young Republicans League in Newton with the son of [the] Massachusetts Governor, and I have the respect and admiration of my community and I am sure I have the respect and admiration of the 25 lawyers or so in Hale & Dorr."

I said, "Fred, I just don't think I am going to ask you to work on the case. If I do, one of these days that will come out and go over national television and it will just hurt like the dickens."

So, Senator, I asked him to go back to Boston.

Little did I dream you could be so reckless and so cruel as to do an injury to that lad. It is true he is still with Hale & Dorr. It is true that he will continue to be with Hale & Dorr. It is, I regret to

"I HAVE HERE IN MY HAND--"

In his anticommunist crusade, McCarthy tampered with the evidence he presented, in one case cropping a photograph to create a false impression and in another case offering as evidence a faked letter. In the Army–McCarthy hearings, the public saw how McCarthy misused and fabricated evidence in his slanderous campaign.

say, equally true that I fear he shall always bear a scar needlessly inflicted by you. If it were in my power to forgive you for your reckless cruelty, I will do so. I like to think I am a gentleman, but your forgiveness will have to come from someone other than me.

Senator McCARTHY. Mr. Chairman.

Senator MUNDT. Senator McCarthy?

Senator McCARTHY. May I say that Mr. Welch talks about this being cruel and reckless. He was just baiting; he has been baiting Mr. Cohn here for hours, requesting that Mr. Cohn, before sundown, get out of any department anyone of Government who is serving the Communist cause.

I just give this man's record, and I want to say, Mr. Welch, that it has been labeled long before he became a member, as early as 1944——

Mr. WELCH. Senator, may we not drop this? We know he belonged to the Lawyers Guild, and Mr. Cohn nods his head at me. I did you, I think, no personal injury, Mr. Cohn.

Mr. COHN. No, sir.

Mr. WELCH. I meant to do you no personal injury, and if I did, I beg your pardon.

Let us not assassinate this lad further, Senator. You have done enough. Have you no sense of decency, sir, at long last? Have you left no sense of decency?

McCarthy had ridden roughshod over the Senate for years, with only occasional voices raised in protest. Earlier, in 1950, Senator Margaret Chase Smith of Maine and six other Republicans had signed a "Declaration of Conscience" criticizing McCarthy's methods, but it had done little good. After the Army–McCarthy hearings, the Senate was more willing to take a stand. In mid-1954, Senator Ralph Flanders of Vermont introduced a motion of censure. A select committee examined the issue and recommended censure, but other Republicans, who had long supported their colleague, balked. They finally agreed on December 2, 1954, by a vote of more than 3 to 1, to a lesser penalty, a resolution to condemn McCarthy. This finally broke McCarthy's power. He died in mid-1957.

Resolved, That the Senator from Wisconsin, Mr. McCARTHY, failed to cooperate with the Subcommittee on Privileges and Elections of the Senate Committee on Rules and Administration in clearing up matters referred to that subcommittee which concerned his conduct as a Senator and affected the honor of the Senate and, instead, repeatedly abused the subcommittee and its

Declaration of Conscience

In a speech to the Senate on June 1, 1950, Senator Margaret Chase Smith said: "The United States Senate has long enjoyed worldwide respect as the greatest deliberative body in the world. But recently that deliberative character has too often been debased to the level of a forum of hate and character assassination sheltered by the shield of congressional immunity." The "Declaration of Conscience" she then read stated: "It is high time that we all stopped being tools and victims of totalitarian techniques—techniques that, if continued here unchecked, will surely end what we have come to cherish as the American way of life."

"*You must remember,*" remarked the King, "*or I'll have you executed.*"

Cartoonist Walt Kelly, creator of the Pogo comic strip, used his artistic talent to caricature Joseph McCarthy. In 1953 he created the character Simple J. Malarkey, an evil wildcat, with dark eyebrows and a five-o'clock shadow that mirrored McCarthy's features. In 1954, Kelly used Malarkey to parody the Army–McCarthy hearings.

members who were trying to carry out assigned duties, thereby obstructing the constitutional processes of the Senate, and that this conduct of the Senator from Wisconsin, Mr. McCARTHY, is contrary to senatorial traditions and is hereby condemned.

SEC. 2. The Senator from Wisconsin, Mr. McCARTHY, in writing to chairman of the Select Committee To Study Censure Charges . . . charging three members of the select committee with "deliberate deception" and "fraud" for failing to disqualify themselves; in stating to the press on November 4, 1954, that the special Senate session that was to begin November 8, 1954, was a "lynch party"; in repeatedly describing this special Senate session as a "lynch bee" in a nationwide television and radio show on November 7, 1954; in stating to the public press on November 13, 1954, that the chairman of the select committee . . . was guilty of "the most unusual, most cowardly thing I've heard of". . . and in characterizing the said committee as the "unwitting handmaiden," "involuntary agent," and "attorneys in fact" of the Communist Party and in charging that the said committee in writing its report "imitated Communist methods—that it distorted, misrepresented, and omitted in its effort to manufacture a plausible rationalization" in support of its recommendations to the Senate, . . . acted contrary to senatorial ethics and tended to bring the Senate into dishonor and disrepute, to obstruct the constitutional processes of the Senate, and to impair its dignity; and such conduct is hereby condemned.

Chapter Three

To the Brink

During the 1950s and 1960s, the United States found itself involved in cold war confrontations around the world. The basic framework of containing communism, established in the years following World War II, continued to shape U.S. foreign policy as the nation responded to challenges in all parts of the globe. Dwight D. Eisenhower (Ike), elected President in 1952, was as much a cold warrior as his predecessor, Harry Truman. Like Truman, Eisenhower sought to prevent the Soviet Union from spreading its influence worldwide. At the same time, he wanted to keep defense spending from escalating out of control and to avoid unnecessary confrontations with the Russians where the nation's immediate interests were not at stake. Ike extricated the United States from the now-stalemated Korean War, yet still found the nation engaged in armed conflicts in other parts of Asia, as well as in Latin America and the Middle East.

John F. Kennedy, elected to the Presidency in 1960, continued the same basic approach as Eisenhower. He, too, subscribed to the policy of containment and insisted on the predominance of U.S. interests. But the youthful Kennedy wanted to be more of an activist than his elderly predecessor and soon became involved in even more serious confrontations, particularly in a near-cataclysmic missile crisis in Cuba. For a few days in 1962, the United States—and the rest of the world—faced the very real threat of nuclear war.

Throughout these decades, the cold war dominated all phases of American life. Nuclear weapons were a constant source of anxiety, as the atomic bombs that had devastated Hiroshima and Nagasaki in Japan gave way to hydrogen bombs that threatened to destroy the world. Military decisions had profound economic consequences, because money spent on foreign policy initiatives meant that there was correspondingly less for enterprises at home. And even though Senator Joseph McCarthy's anticommunist crusade, described in the last chapter, ran out of steam after the Army–McCarthy hearings of 1954, the cold war continued to have a powerful—and not always positive—impact on the lives of most Americans.

Some worried Americans built fall-out shelters in the 1950s to protect themselves from the radioactive residue from a nuclear blast. This sign alerted people that a shelter was nearby.

President Dwight D. Eisenhower, shown here with his wife Mamie, shared the cold war attitudes of his fellow Americans. Like Truman, he believed that communism was a monolithic force sweeping the globe that had to be contained at all costs.

Eisenhower's view of the Soviet Union was much like Truman's. During the 1952 campaign, in his first major foreign policy speech, Ike spoke of the Soviet totalitarian system as "a tyranny that is brutal in its primitiveness. . . a tyranny that has brought thousands, millions of people into slave camps and is attempting to make all humankind its chattel," and he continued to articulate this view throughout his Presidency.

Eisenhower's Inaugural Address

Eisenhower was a committed cold warrior. He had defended the United States as head of the victorious Allied forces in Europe during World War II and was dedicated to maintaining America's position of dominance in the postwar years. As Democrats competed with Republicans in asserting their anticommunist credentials, Eisenhower made it clear that he would stand up to the Chinese as well as the Russians to avoid any infringement of the policies of the United States. His rhetoric in his inaugural address of early 1953 rang with his intention of defending U.S. interests around the world.

The world and we have passed the midway point of a century of continuing challenge. We sense with all our faculties that forces of good and evil are massed and armed and opposed as rarely before in history. . . .

In the swift rush of great events, we find ourselves groping to know the full sense and meaning of these times in which we live. In our quest of understanding, we beseech God's guidance. We summon all our knowledge of the past and we scan all signs of the future. We bring all our wit and all our will to meet the question:

How far have we come in man's long pilgrimage from darkness toward the light? Are we nearing the light—a day of freedom and of peace for all mankind? Or are the shadows of another night closing in upon us?

Great as are the preoccupations absorbing us at home, concerned as we are with matters that deeply affect our livelihood today and our vision of the future, each of these domestic problems is dwarfed by, and often even created by, this question that involves all humankind. . . .

At such a time in history, we who are free must proclaim our faith. This faith is the abiding creed of our fathers. It is our faith in the deathless dignity of man, governed by eternal moral and natural laws.

This faith defines our full view of life. It establishes, beyond debate, those gifts of the Creator that are man's inalienable rights, and that make all men equal in His sight. . . .

The enemies of this faith know no god but force, no devotion but its use. They tutor men in treason. They feed upon the hunger of others. Whatever defies them, they torture, especially the truth.

Here, then, is joined no argument between slightly differing philosophies. This conflict strikes directly at the faith of our fathers and the lives of our sons. No principle or treasure that we hold, from the spiritual knowledge of our free schools and churches to the creative magic of free labor and capital, nothing lies safely beyond the reach of this struggle.

Freedom is pitted against slavery; lightness against the dark. . . .

Liberation of Captive Peoples

Eisenhower's secretary of state, John Foster Dulles, was a devout Presbyterian who hated atheistic communism. He too saw the cold war as a moral struggle between good and evil and believed the Truman administration's policy of containment did not go far enough. He proposed instead the liberation of peoples who found themselves under the control of the Soviet Union. Dulles developed this idea in mid-1952, during the Presidential campaign, in an article in *Life* magazine. Seeking to shape U.S. foreign policy even before his appointment as secretary of state, he played a major role in the Republican administration's conduct of diplomacy in the 1950s.

Soviet Communism confronts our nation with its gravest peril. To meet its long-term strategy of encirclement and strangulation, we have adopted a series of emergency measures which are fantastically costly not only in money but in their warping of our American way of life.

No one would begrudge the cost of what we are doing if, in fact, it was adequate and was ending the peril, and if there was no better way. Actually, our policies are *inadequate* in scope. They are *not* ending the peril. There *is* a better way.

The costs of our present policies are perilously high in money, in freedom and in friendships. . . .

There are times when nations have to pay such high costs to win a victory and end a peril. We know that from the last two World Wars. But today our policies are not designed to win a victory conclusively.

If you will think back over the past six years, you will see that our policies have largely involved emergency action to try to "contain" Soviet Communism by checking it here or blocking it there. We are not working, sacrificing and spending in order to be able to live *without* this peril—but to be able to live *with* it, presumably forever. . . .

Eisenhower sometimes bristled at the contention that John Foster Dulles was the architect of U.S. foreign policy and never doubted his own role in calling the shots. While acknowledging Dulles's background and influence, Ike once commented, ". . . I'll be immodest and say that there's only one man I know who has seen *more* of the world and talked with more people and *knows* more than he does—and that's *me*."

Secretary of State John Foster Dulles (right) was a moralist who believed that it was essential to contain "Godless communism." For him, the cold war was a devout crusade in which the forces of good were locked in combat against the forces of evil. He met with Anthony Eden, British Secretary of State, in 1956.

The Soviet Union worried about the new American policy. Soviet leader Nikita Khrushchev, who consolidated his power after Stalin's death in March 1953, later recalled: "In the days leading up to Stalin's death, we believed that America would invade the Soviet Union and we would go to war. Stalin trembled at this prospect. How he quivered! He was afraid of war. He knew that we were weaker than the United States. We had only a handful of nuclear weapons, while America had a large arsenal of nuclear arms. Of course, in other areas—convention forces and ground forces—we had the advantage."

We want, for ourselves and the other free nations, a maximum deterrent at a bearable cost. Local defense will always be important. But there is no local defense which alone will contain the mighty land power of the Communist world. Local defenses must be reinforced by the further deterrent of massive retaliatory power. . . . The way to deter aggression is for the free community to be willing and able to respond vigorously at places and with means of its own choosing.

—Secretary of State John Foster Dulles, supporting the new policy of reliance on nuclear arms in 1954

Our present negative policies will never end the type of sustained offensive which Soviet Communism is mounting; they will never end the peril nor bring relief from the exertions which devour our economic, political and moral vitals. Ours are treadmill policies which, at best, might perhaps keep us in the same place until we drop exhausted. . . .

There is one solution and only one: that is for the free world to develop the will and organize the means to retaliate instantly against open aggression by Red armies, so that, if it occurred anywhere, we could and would strike back where it hurts, by means of our own choosing. . . .

Once the free world has established a military defense, it can undertake what has been too long delayed—a political offense. . . .

Consider the situation of the 20-odd non-Western nations which are next door to the Soviet world. These exposed nations feel that they have been put into the "expendable" class, condemned in perpetuity to be the ramparts against which the angry waves of Soviet Communism will constantly hurl themselves. They are expected to live precariously, permanently barred from areas with which they normally should have trade, commerce and cultural relations. They cannot be enthusiastic about policies which would merely perpetuate so hazardous and uncomfortable a position. Today they live close to despair because the United States, the historic leader of the forces of freedom, seems dedicated to the negative policy of "containment" and "stalemate."

As a matter of fact, some highly competent work is being done, at one place or another, to promote liberation. Obviously such activities do not lend themselves to public exposition. But liberation from the yoke of Moscow will not occur for a very long time, and courage in neighboring lands will not be sustained, *unless the United States makes it publicly known that it wants and expects liberation to occur.* The mere statement of that wish and expectation would change, in an electrifying way, the mood of the captive peoples. It would put heavy new burdens on the jailers and create new opportunities for liberation.

Another priority of the Eisenhower years was to find a military approach that would not bankrupt the United States. The defense budget had become swollen in 1950–53 during the Korean War , and Ike, who wanted to balance the budget, sought to cut back on heavy defense costs without compromising security. He therefore asked his Joint Chiefs of Staff to survey the nation's strategic requirements and balance the various military, diplomatic, and fiscal factors. After

some debate, the Joint Chiefs declared that they could control costs and maintain U.S. security by depending less on conventional forces and more on nuclear weapons. Eisenhower accepted their strategic recommendation, which was incorporated into a National Security Council directive in the fall of 1953.

The new policy came to be called both the "New Look" and "Massive Retaliation." It would, people said, give "more bang for the buck."

. . . 9. In the face of the Soviet threat, the security of the United States requires:

a. Development and maintenance of:

(1) A strong military posture, with emphasis on the capability of inflicting massive retaliatory damage by offensive striking power;

(2) U.S. and allied forces in readiness to move rapidly initially to counter aggression by Soviet bloc forces and to hold vital areas and lines of communication; and

(3) A mobilization base, and its protection against crippling damage, adequate to insure victory in the event of general war.

b. Maintenance of a sound, strong and growing economy, capable of providing through the operation of free institutions,

That was what kept peace in the world. That and that alone, I am sure is what kept peace in the world. And all the rest of these soldiers and sailors and submariners and everything else, comparatively speaking, you could drop in the ocean, and it wouldn't make too much difference.

—Secretary of the Treasury George Humphrey, applauding the new policy of "Massive Retaliation"

Dwight Eisenhower was eager to find a cost-effective strategy to defend the United States in the cold war. Working with the Joint Chiefs of Staff, the top-ranking officers in each military branch—shown here with a globe—he endorsed the policy of "Massive Retaliation," which placed far greater reliance than before on nuclear weapons.

the strength described in *a* above over the long pull and of rapidly and effectively changing to full mobilization.

c. Maintenance of morale and free institutions and the willingness of the U.S. people to support the measures necessary for national security. . . .

11. Within the free world, only the United States can provide and maintain, for a period of years to come, the atomic capability to counterbalance Soviet atomic power. Thus, sufficient atomic weapons and effective means of delivery are indispensable for U.S. security. Moreover, in the face of Soviet atomic power, defense of the continental United States becomes vital to effective security: to protect our striking force, our mobilization base, and our people. Such atomic capability is also a major contribution to the security of our allies, as well as of this country. . . .

39. *b.* (1) In the event of hostilities, the United States will consider nuclear weapons to be as available for use as other munitions. . . .

The Domino Theory

One other concept also guided U.S. foreign policy in the 1950s. Eisenhower firmly believed that the fall of one nation to communism would pave the way for others to fall in turn. This seemed particularly true in Indochina, where a number of countries were at risk. If Indochina was lost, Burma, Thailand, and Indonesia would likely be next, after which Japan, Formosa (present-day Taiwan), and the Philippines would be at risk, and there might be threats to Australia and New Zealand as well. At a press conference in the spring of 1954, Ike compared the Southeast Asia situation to a row of falling dominoes, and the resulting "domino theory" came to justify a stalwart anticommunist stance. In response to a question about the strategic importance of Indochina to the free world, Eisenhower replied:

You have, of course, both the specific and the general when you talk about such things.

First of all, you have the specific value of a locality in its production of materials that the world needs.

Then you have the possibility that many human beings pass under a dictatorship that is inimical to the free world.

Finally, you have the broader considerations that might follow what you would call the "falling domino" principle. You have a

Several weeks after using the domino analogy, Eisenhower came up with another in a speech about Indochina to the U.S. Chamber of Commerce: "We have here a sort of cork in the bottle, the bottle being the great area that includes Indonesia, Burma, Thailand, all of the surrounding areas of Asia with its hundreds of millions of people, and its geographical location that controls lines of communication, to say nothing of the great products of the region, some of which we must have."

row of dominoes set up, you knock over the first one, and what will happen to the last one is the certainty that it will go over very quickly. So you could have a beginning of a disintegration that would have the most profound influences.

Now, with respect to the first one, two of the items from this particular area that the world uses are tin and tungsten. They are very important. There are others, of course, the rubber plantations and so on.

Then with respect to more people passing under this domination, Asia, after all, has already lost some 450 million of its peoples to the Communist dictatorship, and we simply can't afford greater losses.

But when we come to the possible sequence of events, the loss of Indochina, of Burma, of Thailand, of the [Indochinese] Peninsula, and Indonesia following, now you begin to talk about areas that not only multiply the disadvantages you suffer through loss of materials, sources of materials, but now you are talking really about millions and millions and millions of people.

Finally, the geographical position achieved thereby does many things. It turns the so-called island defensive chain of Japan, Formosa, of the Philippines and to the southward; it moves in to threaten Australia and New Zealand.

It takes away, in its economic aspects, that region that Japan must have as a trading area or Japan, in turn, will have only one place in the world to go—that is, toward the Communist areas in order to live.

So, the possible consequences of the loss are just incalculable to the free world.

The cold war affected U.S. policy toward countries around the world. In Egypt, a major confrontation threatened international stability. When Egypt's General Gamel Abdel Nasser seized the British-controlled Suez Canal and closed it to Israeli shipping, a combined British, French, and Israeli force invaded Egypt. The United States, eager to avoid edging Nasser into the Russian camp, pushed through a United Nations resolution condemning the attack. Peace was restored, but America's relations with its allies remained frayed.

As the Suez crisis unfolded, there was trouble in Europe as well. The death of Joseph Stalin, the Soviet dictator, in 1953 led to a loosening up in the Soviet Union. When his successor, Nikita Khrushchev, suggested in 1956 that tight restrictions on satellite nations might be relaxed, there was

Allies at Odds

Eisenhower was furious at the attack on Egypt, for the British and French had earlier assured him they would not rely on force. He was particularly angry at British Prime Minister Anthony Eden, whom he had known since World War II. "Bombs, by God," he roared, "What does Anthony think he's doing?" When informed that paratroopers were about to land near the canal, he declared, "I think it is the biggest error of our time, outside of losing China."

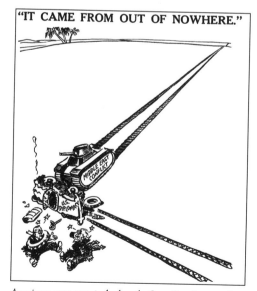

Americans were surprised when the Suez Canal crisis of 1956 threatened to erupt into a full-scale war. This cartoon by Herblock, one of the nation's best-known political cartoonists, shows the impact of being caught unaware. A tank labeled "Middle East Conflict" has smashed the vehicle of "U.S. Diplomacy."

Our goal in Hungary was to support progressivism and to assist the people's transition from capitalism to Socialism. The enemies of Socialism had the opposite goal: wherever a Socialist way of life had been achieved, they wanted to liquidate it, to suppress the working class, and to restore capitalism.

By helping the Hungarian people to crush the counterrevolutionary mutiny we have prevented the enemy from impairing the unity of the entire Socialist camp, rigorously tested during the Hungarian events.

—Nikita S. Khrushchev, Soviet leader at the time of the Hungarian uprising

Revolution is inevitable in Latin America. The people are angry. They are shackled to the past with bonds of ignorance, injustice, and poverty. And they no longer accept as universal or inevitable the oppressive prevailing order.

—Milton Eisenhower, the President's brother and advisor, at the time of the Cuban revolution

Trouble for the communists erupted in Eastern Europe in 1956. As a Russian-type tank guarded a bank in Poznan, Poland, rioting in the streets by antigovernment forces continued, and thousands of Polish workers threatened to remain on strike if the government did not release rebel leaders.

rioting in the streets in Poland and Hungary by students and workers eager for freedom. Khrushchev finally responded by sending tanks and soldiers to put down the revolt. In all, 40,000 Hungarians died, and another 150,000 fled to Western Europe and the United States. Containment—not liberation—remained the basis of U.S. foreign policy.

The cold war also affected foreign relations in Latin America. In 1954, afraid that communist influence might be growing, the United States ordered CIA support for a coup that ousted the elected government of Colonel Jacobo Arbenz Guzmán and replaced it with a military dictatorship that restored property to the United Fruit Company, which Guzmán had nationalized. Latin Americans throughout the hemisphere were angry at this intervention by the United States. Seeking to respond to eager demands for social reform, they were often sympathetic to challenges to the existing capitalist order, whatever the reaction of their powerful northern neighbor. Five years later, they applauded the successful revolution of Fidel Castro that overthrew a dictatorial regime in Cuba. At first the Eisenhower administration accepted the Cuban revolution, but after Cuba confiscated U.S. property it severed diplomatic ties. That action led Cuba to turn to the Soviet Union for support as the 1960s began.

Meanwhile, the cold war had a profound impact on social patterns in the United States as well. In the post–World War II period, Americans felt a renewed sense of religious commitment and returned to their houses of worship in record numbers. Church membership doubled in the years

In 1954, The U.S. Central Intelligence Agency assisted Guatemalan military leaders in overthrowing the democratically elected government of Colonel Jacobo Arbenz Guzmán. The United States was concerned that Guatemala was sympathetic to the Soviet Union and hostile to American business interests. Flying over the square in Guatemala City, this small plane dropped propoganda leaflets on a crowd listening to a political speech.

between 1945 and 1970. One reason for this religious resurgence was a feeling of relief at having survived the war successfully. But another important reason was a desire to challenge the "godless communism" people felt was undermining American values and threatening the moral fabric of the United States.

Evangelist Billy Graham was in the forefront of the religious campaign against communism in the 1950s and 1960s. Preaching his fiery message at revivals and on the radio and television, he urged sinners to embrace God and thus save their nation from the frightening perils of the communist threat. In 1954, Graham published the central arguments he used in his sermons in a widely read article entitled "Satan's Religion" in the right-wing magazine *American Mercury*.

The Communist revolution that was born in the hearts of [Karl] Marx and [Friedrich] Engels in the middle of the nineteenth century is not going to give up or retreat. No amount of words at the United Nations or peace conferences in the Far East is going to change the mind of Communism. It is here to stay. It is a battle to the death—either Communism must die, or Christianity must die, because it is actually a battle between Christ and anti-Christ. . . .

Billy Graham was a powerful preacher. In one sermon, he thundered: "Unless America at this tragic hour is willing to turn to Jesus Christ and be cleansed by the blood of Christ and know the regenerating power of the Holy Spirit, Christ will never save the nation." And how, he asked rhetorically, would America be saved? His answer: "When you make your decision for Jesus Christ, it is America making her decision through you."

Americans in the 1950s became increasingly concerned about the challenge communism posed to Christianity. As evangelists preached that embracing Christianity was the appropriate way to contain communism, some artists used cartoons like this one—showing a cross at one pole and a Russian hammer and sickle at the other—to illustrate the tremendous distance between Western religion and Soviet ideology.

So fanatical and ruthless are these disciples of Lucifer that in thirty years they have slaughtered millions of innocent persons and stand prepared with poised weapons to kill millions more in an all-out effort to spread their doctrines to the ends of the earth.

The mysterious pull of this satanic religion is so strong that it has caused some citizens of America to become traitorous, betraying a benevolent land which had showered them with blessings innumerable. It has attracted some of our famous entertainers, some of our keenest politicians, and some of our outstanding educators.

With the forces of Communism now in possession of modern nuclear weapons and modern, fast, powerful planes for pin-point delivery of death-dealing bombs, it behooves Americans to gird on the whole armor of God that we may be able to stand in the evil day. . . .

The greatest need in America today is for men and women to be born again by the Holy Spirit, by repenting of their sins, and receiving Christ as Saviour. The greatest and most effective weapon against Communism today is to be born again Christian. . . .

Unstable Peace

The cold war invaded other corners of American life as well. Homosexuals faced charges that they were security risks, who could not be trusted. Civil rights leaders found themselves the targets of attack. Martin Luther King, Jr., who first gained public attention in the Montgomery bus boycott of 1955 and 1956 and became the preeminent black leader of the era, experienced relentless surveillance by the Federal Bureau of Investigation (FBI), for bureau head J. Edgar Hoover believed that King was a communist tool. Any challenge to the existing social order faced the charge that it was inspired by communists at home and abroad.

Americans who became concerned about the perils of nuclear war found themselves similarly charged with aiding the Soviet side. Nuclear testing was a major enterprise in the 1950s, but its critics pressed on nonetheless. For one thing, as atomic weapons based on fission—the splitting of the atom—gave way to thermonuclear bombs based on fusion—the combining of atomic elements in a reaction like that on the surface of the sun—weapons became more lethal than ever. For another, in 1954 the public became aware of a new menace: fallout. The radioactive residue of a test in the Pacific, in

The cold war intruded on the civil rights movement. The Reverend Martin Luther King, Jr., stands in front of a desegregated bus in Montgomery, Alabama, in 1956, after leading the bus boycott there. One of the most prominent civil rights leaders in the United States, King found himself facing an FBI investigation on the grounds that any effort to challenge traditional social patterns at home assisted the communist cause.

which the United States exploded its first operational hydrogen bomb, spread more widely than expected to contaminate the crew members of a Japanese fishing vessel called the *Fukuryu Maru* (Lucky Dragon). Many of them became sick and one died.

Some critics marshaled scientific arguments to demand an end to nuclear testing, but others used humor to make the same point. Songwriter Tom Lehrer was one of the most creative critics. A mathematician who wrote songs in his spare time and accompanied himself on the piano, Lehrer poked fun at all kinds of targets, including the U.S. government's atomic energy policy. In a number of songs he pointed out the consequences of testing and the perils of nuclear war. In 1953, in his first album, in "The Wild West Is Where I Want to Be," he sang about the issue of radioactivity generated by the tests of the Atomic Energy Commission (AEC), noting in one verse the need for lead-lined undershorts:

As worldwide attention focused on the *Lucky Dragon*, AEC chairman Lewis Strauss at first asserted that the ship was not a legitimate operation but a "Red spy outfit." He then added, "If I were the Reds, I would fill the oceans all over the world with radio-active fish. It would be so easy to do!" Despite that attempt to deflect criticism, the U.S. ambassador to Japan apologized to the Japanese, and the United States eventually paid $2 million to compensate the Japanese for their losses.

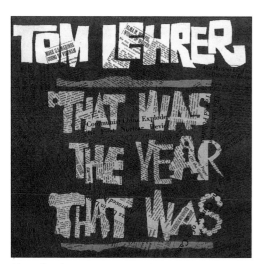

Tom Lehrer kept writing songs in the 1960s, and continued to sing about the nuclear threat. His 1965 album That Was the Year That Was included "So Long, Mom," about the use of the bomb in the next war we might fight, and "Who's Next?," about nuclear proliferation.

Along the trail you'll find me lopin'
Where the spaces are wide open,
In the land of the old A.E.C.
Where the scenery's attractive,
And the air is radioactive,
Oh, the wild west is where I want to be.

'Mid the sagebrush and the cactus
I'll watch the fellers practice
Droppin' bombs through the clean desert breeze.
I'll have on my sombrero,
And of course I'll wear a pair o'
Levis over my lead B.V.D.'s.

Six years later, Lehrer took up the atomic threat again in his second album. In "We Will All Go Together When We Go," he pointed to the massive consequences of a nuclear blast:

And we will all go together when we go,
Ev'ry Hottentot and ev'ry Eskimo.
When the air becomes uranious,
We will all go simultaneous,
Yes, we will all go together
When we all go together,
Yes, we all will go together when we go.

As Eisenhower prepared to leave office in early 1961, he was concerned about continuing threats to world peace. He had managed to defend U.S. interests and maintain the delicate cold war balance while avoiding large-scale military involvement in any major wars. As the nuclear arsenals in both the United States and the Soviet Union grew ever larger, Ike had followed the Russian example and approved a voluntary testing moratorium that lasted for several years. Yet he still recognized the fragility of the unstable peace and worried about the demand for military development that was affecting the nation at home and abroad. In his farewell address, he warned of the dangers of a growing military-industrial complex that sometimes took on a life of its own.

Throughout America's adventure in free government, our basic purposes have been to keep the peace; to foster progress in human achievement, and to enhance liberty, dignity and integrity among people and among nations. To strive for less would be unworthy of a free and religious people. Any failure traceable to arrogance, or our lack of comprehension or readiness to sacrifice would inflict upon us grievous hurt both at home and abroad.

Progress toward these noble goals is persistently threatened by the conflict now engulfing the world. It commands our whole attention, absorbs our very beings. We face a hostile ideology— global in scope, atheistic in character, ruthless in purpose, and insidious in method. Unhappily the danger it poses promises to be of indefinite duration. To meet it successfully, there is called for, not so much the emotional and transitory sacrifices of crisis, but rather those which enable us to carry forward steadily, surely, and without complaint the burdens of a prolonged and complex struggle—with liberty the stake. Only thus shall we remain, despite every provocation, on our charted course toward permanent peace and human betterment. . . .

The cold war extended even into space. On October 4, 1957, the Soviet Union put the world's first artificial satellite, named Sputnik (fellow traveler), into orbit around the earth. Sputnik weighed 184 pounds and traveled in an elliptical orbit, ranging in altitude from about 140 to 560 miles, that took one and a half hours to complete. Americans were stunned, for they prided themselves on their technological superiority. Soon another Soviet satellite—this one weighing 1,120 pounds and carrying a dog—went into orbit, and another soon followed. The United States finally managed to loft a number of smaller satellites into orbit, but it remained embarrassed at having come off second best. Sputnik fascinated people around the world, including these Soviet citizens in Moscow gazing at a model of Sputnik I.

A Cold War Childhood

The month of my twelfth birthday. . .
was also the October when the Russians
launched the first artificial satellite into orbit.
I remember hearing over the radio the signals
beamed down from *Sputnik I*, like the chirping
of crickets in the autumn fields. However
worried the grown-ups might have been by
this proof of Soviet wizardry, it lifted my
heart, because rockets and satellites promised
to carry our questions out into the heavens.
Where did the universe come from? Is anyone or anything in charge? Why are we here,
alive and thinking? Are we going anywhere,
or are we just wandering around, passing the
time until we die? And when we die, is that
the end, or does some part of us survive?

—Scott Russell Sanders, *Hunting for Hope:
A Father's Journey*

A vital element in keeping the peace is our military establishment. Our arms must be mighty, ready for instant action, so that
no potential aggressor may be tempted to risk his own destruction.

Our military organization today bears little relation to that
known by any of my predecessors in peacetime, or indeed by the
fighting men of World War II or Korea.

Until the latest of our world conflicts, the United States had
no armaments industry. American makers of plowshares could,
with time and as required, make swords as well. But now we can
no longer risk emergency improvisation of national defense; we
have been compelled to create a permanent armaments industry
of vast proportions. Added to this, three and a half million men
and women are directly engaged in the defense establishment. We
annually spend on military security more than the net income of
all United States corporations.

This conjunction of an immense military establishment and a
large arms industry is new in the American experience. The total
influence—economic, political, even spiritual—is felt in every
city, every State house, every office of the Federal government.
We recognize the imperative need for this development. Yet we
must not fail to comprehend its grave implications. Our toil,
resources and livelihood are all involved; so is the very structure
of our society.

In the councils of government, we must guard against the
acquisition of unwarranted influence, whether sought or
unsought, by the military-industrial complex. The potential for
the disastrous rise of misplaced power exists and will persist.

We must never let the weight of this combination endanger
our liberties or democratic processes. We should take nothing for
granted. Only an alert and knowledgeable citizenry can compel
the proper meshing of the huge industrial and military machinery
of defense with our peaceful methods and goals, so that security
and liberty may prosper together.

Akin to, and largely responsible for the sweeping changes in
our industrial-military posture, has been the technological revolution during recent decades.

In this revolution, research has become central; it also
becomes more formalized, complex, and costly. A steadily
increasing share is conducted for, by, or at the direction of the
Federal government.

Today, the solitary inventor, tinkering in his shop, has been over-
shadowed by task forces of scientists in laboratories and testing

fields. In the same fashion, the free university, historically the fountainhead of free ideas and scientific discovery, has experienced a revolution in the conduct of research. Partly because of the huge costs involved, a government contract becomes virtually a substitute for intellectual curiosity. For every old blackboard there are now hundreds of new electric computers.

The prospect of domination of the nation's scholars by Federal employment, project allocations, and the power of money is ever present—and is gravely to be regarded.

Yet, in holding scientific research and discovery in respect, as we should, we must also be alert to the equal and opposite danger that public policy could itself become the captive of a scientific-technological elite.

It is the task of statesmanship to mold, to balance, and to integrate these and other forces, new and old, within the principles of our democratic system—ever aiming toward the supreme goals of our free society. . . .

Kennedy's Inaugural Address

John F. Kennedy, who followed Eisenhower in the White House, was as much a cold warrior as his predecessor. He was part of the bipartisan consensus in the post–World War II years that was determined to stand firm in the face of the Soviet threat, which meant taking any action necessary to protect U.S. interests. At the same time, Kennedy was more of an activist than Eisenhower. At 43, as the youngest man ever elected President, he wanted to use his energy and enthusiasm to fulfill his campaign pledge to get the country moving again. He hoped to take the necessary steps to promote prosperity at home, but he was even more interested in the world of foreign affairs. Wanting to take bold action to stand up to the Soviets, he broadcast his intentions in ringing terms in his inaugural address.

We observe today not a victory of party but a celebration of freedom—symbolizing an end as well as a beginning—signifying renewal as well as change. For I have sworn before you and Almighty God the same solemn oath our forebears prescribed nearly a century and three quarters ago.

The world is very different now. For man holds in his mortal hands the power to abolish all forms of human poverty and all

Man on the Moon

The space race continued. In a message to Congress in the spring of 1961, President John F. Kennedy declared: "I believe that this nation should commit itself to achieving the goal, before this decade is out, of landing a man on the moon and returning him safely to the earth. No single space project in this period will be more impressive to mankind, or more important for the long-range exploration of space; and none will be so difficult or expensive to accomplish." The United States made good on this commitment in 1969.

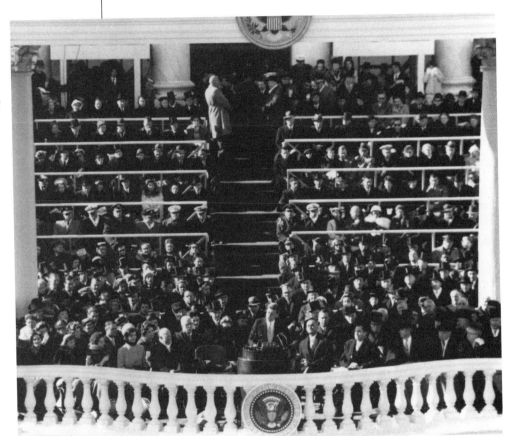

President John F. Kennedy issued a ringing challenge in his inaugural address in 1961. Pointing to the dangers to freedom the United States faced in the cold war, he asked all Americans to do whatever they could to help defend their values around the world.

forms of human life. And yet the same revolutionary beliefs for which our forebears fought are still at issue around the globe—the belief that the rights of man come not from the generosity of the state but from the hand of God.

We dare not forget today that we are the heirs of that first revolution. Let the word go forth from this time and place, to friend and foe alike, that the torch has been passed to a new generation of Americans—born in this century, tempered by war, disciplined by a hard and bitter peace, proud of our ancient heritage—and unwilling to witness or permit the slow undoing of those human rights to which this nation has always been committed, and to which we are committed today at home and around the world.

Let every nation know, whether it wishes us well or ill, that we shall pay any price, bear any burden, meet any hardship, support any friend, oppose any foe to assure the survival and the success of liberty.

This much we pledge—and more. . . .

To those nations who would make themselves our adversary, we offer not a pledge but a request: that both sides begin anew the quest for peace, before the dark powers of destruction unleashed

K ennedy took a hard line toward the Soviet Union. During the Presidential campaign of 1960, in a speech at the Mormon Tabernacle in Salt Lake City, he declared: "The enemy is the communist system itself— implacable, insatiable, unceasing in its drive for world domination. For this is not a struggle for the supremacy of arms alone—it is also a struggle for supremacy between two conflicting ideologies: Freedom under God versus ruthless, godless tyranny."

by science engulf all humanity in planned or accidental self-destruction. . . .

So let us begin anew—remembering on both sides that civility is not a sign of weakness, and sincerity is always subject to proof. Let us never negotiate out of fear. But let us never fear to negotiate. . . .

In the long history of the world, only a few generations have been granted the role of defending freedom in its hour of maximum danger. I do not shrink from this responsibility—I welcome it. I do not believe that any of us would exchange places with any other people or any other generation. The energy, the faith, the devotion which we bring to this endeavor will light our country and all who serve it—and the glow from that fire can truly light the world.

And so, my fellow Americans: ask not what your country can do for you—ask what you can do for your country.

My fellow citizens of the world: ask not what America will do for you, but what together we can do for the freedom of man.

Finally, whether you are citizens of America or citizens of the world, ask of us here the same high standards of strength and sacrifice which we ask of you. With a good conscience our only sure reward, with history the final judge of our deeds, let us go forth to lead the land we love, asking His blessing and His help, but knowing that here on earth God's work must truly be our own.

Bay of Pigs

After he was elected President, Kennedy learned that the CIA had been secretly training anti-Castro exiles in Guatemala to storm the central coast of Cuba at the Bay of Pigs. The U.S. planners hoped that this invasion would lead to an uprising of the Cuban people against Castro and eliminate communist influence on this island only 90 miles away from the United States.

Reactions to the proposed invasion were mixed. The Joint Chiefs of Staff went along with the CIA, agreeing that the United States would provide logistical support to an invasion by Cuban exiles. Marine Corps commandant David Shoup urged caution, however, arguing that Cuba was a large island and would not be taken with ease. As newspapers got wind of the proposal and began forecasting an invasion, some members of Congress voiced their reservations about the plan.

After Fidel Castro seized power in the Cuban revolution of 1959, he allied himself with Soviet leader Nikita Khrushchev (right), who embraced Castro at the United Nations. The Soviet Union's aid to Cuba angered the United States, which resolved to take action to liberate Cuba from Castro's communist leadership.

Unheeded Counsel

J. William Fulbright, chairman of the Senate Foreign Relations Committee, adamantly opposed the invasion. In a memorandum to President Kennedy he wrote: "To give this activity even covert support is of a piece with the hypocrisy and cynicism for which the United States is constantly denouncing the Soviet Union in the United Nations and elsewhere." He concluded by saying that the situation was not desperate: "The Castro regime is a thorn in the flesh; but it is not a dagger in the heart."

The American invasion of Cuba at the Bay of Pigs in 1961 was a failure. Kennedy faced intense criticism for authorizing the attack, and found himself ridiculed in the press. Here a large chicken named "Bay of Pigs" roosts on top of the White House.

Publicly, Kennedy categorically denied any U.S. involvement in the scheme. In a news conference on April 12, 1961, responding to a question about how far the United States might go to support an anti-Castro uprising, he declared that his government would maintain its distance.

First, I want to say that there will not be, under any conditions, an intervention in Cuba by the United States Armed Forces. This government will do everything it possibly can, and I think it can meet its responsibilities, to make sure that there are no Americans involved in any actions inside Cuba. . . .

We do not intend to take any action with respect to the property or other economic interests which America formerly held in Cuba, other than formal and normal negotiations with a free and independent Cuba.

The basic issue in Cuba is not one between the United States and Cuba. It is between the Cubans themselves. I intend to see that we adhere to that principle and as I understand it this administration's attitude is so understood and shared by the anti-Castro exiles from Cuba in this country.

The invasion took place on April 17 and was an unmitigated disaster. It followed an air strike over Cuba two days earlier, in which U.S. planes based in Nicaragua, painted to look as though they were stolen Cuban planes, failed to knock out Castro's air force but alerted him that an attack was imminent. As the exile troops sought to land and go ashore, Castro had little difficulty holding them off. Though urged to use American planes for air cover, Kennedy refused to authorize another strike, recognizing that the mission was a hopeless failure. The Cubans followed the lead of Fidel Castro, not that of the expatriate invaders, leaving the United States embarrassingly exposed to the rest of the world for its clumsy efforts to overthrow a sovereign government.

For the United States, the attack was a disaster. It had broken agreements not to interfere in the internal affairs of its hemispheric neighbors and had intervened in a bumbling way, with no sense of restraint. People at home and abroad who had been earlier stirred by Kennedy's ringing rhetoric now questioned his ability to lead. Publicly, in the following speech to the American Society of Newspaper Editors, the President tried to portray the episode as an entirely Cuban affair, despite the evidence of U.S. involvement that was

**visible worldwide. Privately, he accepted personal responsi-
bility for the fiasco and voiced his determination to deal
more effectively with the communist threat in the future.**

The President of a great democracy such as ours, and the editors
of great newspapers such as yours, owe a common obligation to
the people: an obligation to present the facts, to present them
with candor, and to present them in perspective. It is with that
obligation in mind that I have decided in the last 24 hours to discuss briefly at this time the recent events in Cuba.

On that unhappy island, as in so many other arenas of the con-
test for freedom, the news has grown worse instead of better. I
have emphasized before that this was a struggle of Cuban patriots
against a Cuban dictator. While we could not be expected to hide
our sympathies, we made it repeatedly clear that the armed forces
of this country would not intervene in any way.

Any unilateral American intervention, in the absence of an
external attack upon our selves or an ally, would have been contrary to our international obligations. But let the record show that
our restraint is not inexhaustible. Should it ever appear that the
inter-American doctrine of non-interference merely conceals or
excuses a policy of nonaction—if the nations of the Hemisphere
should fail to meet their commitments against outside Communist
penetration—then I want it clearly understood that this Government will not hesitate in meeting its primary obligations which are
to the security of our Nation!

Standing Up to the Soviets

**After the experience of the Bay of Pigs, President Kennedy
was more intent than ever on standing up to the Soviets. A
few months later, in June 1961, he met Russian leader Nikita
Khrushchev for the first time in Vienna, where he faced yet
another crisis. In the years following World War II, Germany
had remained divided into zones occupied by the major
Allied powers, with the city of Berlin likewise divided. Grad-
ually the lines hardened until there were now two separate
German nations: East Germany, controlled by the Soviet
Union; and West Germany, dominated by the Western Allies.
In 1948, when the Soviets had cut off surface travel to West
Berlin, the United States had responded with an airlift to furnish supplies to the city, which lay within East Germany. That
crisis passed, but in 1958 the Soviets again challenged the**

Radical sociologist C. Wright Mills criticized the Bay of Pigs invasion in a
telegram to a Fair Play for Cuba rally in San
Francisco: "Kennedy and company have
returned us to barbarism. . . . I feel a desperate shame for my country. Sorry I cannot be
with you. Were I physically able to do so, I
would at this moment be fighting alongside
Fidel Castro."

Pierre Salinger, Kennedy's press secretary,
later noted that the attack on the Bay of
Pigs was the "least covert military operation
in history" and observed that "The only
information Castro didn't have . . . was the
exact time and place of the invasion."

After returning from his meeting with Khrushchev, in a July 1961 address Kennedy called West Berlin "the great testing place of Western courage and will." The United States, he declared, would not be pushed around: "We do not want to fight—but we have fought before."

postwar pattern, then backed away once more. With Kennedy in office, Khrushchev demanded a peace treaty that would reflect the reality of the division that had occurred. He was concerned with the steady flow of East Germans into West Germany, particularly those passing from East Berlin into West Berlin.

Kennedy, irritated at Khrushchev's demand, on his return home told the American people that he saw it as a prelude to an aggressive communist movement on the continent as a whole. He asked Congress for an increased defense appropriation of more than $3 billion, requested more men for the army, navy, and air force, and tripled the draft calls. He also sought $207 million for a civil defense fallout shelter program.

The Soviets responded by building a huge wall through Berlin. It effectively sealed East Berliners inside the city and alleviated the immediate problem for the Soviets of having East Germans fleeing to the West. For all his rhetoric, there was little Kennedy could do about the wall, which became a vivid example of the divisive impact of the cold war. Two years later, Kennedy used it as a symbol of Western solidarity on a trip to Berlin.

Kennedy met Khrushchev for the first time in Vienna in 1961. Though the two leaders greeted one another amicably, in the discussions that followed Kennedy came off second-best and returned home fearing Soviet designs on all of Europe.

Two thousand years ago the proudest boast was *"civis Romanus sum"* [I am a Roman]. Today, in the world of freedom, the proudest boast is *"Ich bin ein Berliner"* [I am a Berliner].

There are many people in the world who really don't understand, or say they don't, what is the great issue between the free world and the Communist world. Let them come to Berlin. There are some who say that communism is the wave of the future. Let them come to Berlin. And there are some who say in Europe and elsewhere we can work with the Communists. Let them come to Berlin. And there are even a few who say that it is true that communism is an evil system, but it permits us to make economic progress. *Lass' sie nach Berlin kommen.* Let them come to Berlin.

Freedom has many difficulties and democracy is not perfect, but we have never had to put a wall up to keep our people in, to prevent them from leaving us. . . . While the wall is the most obvious and vivid demonstration of the failures of the Communist system, for all the world to see, we take no satisfaction in it, for it is . . . an offense not only against history but an offense against humanity, separating families, dividing husbands and wives and brothers and sisters, and dividing a people who wish to be joined together. . . .

Freedom is indivisible, and when one man is enslaved, all are not free. When all are free, then we can look forward to that day when this city will be joined as one and this country and this great Continent of Europe in a peaceful and hopeful globe. When that day finally comes, as it will, the people of West Berlin can take sober satisfaction in the fact that they were in the front lines for almost two decades.

All free men, wherever they may live, are citizens of Berlin, and, therefore, as a free man, I take pride in the words *"Ich bin ein Berliner."*

The Cuban Missile Crisis

As the Berlin issue intensified, Kennedy faced still another crisis in Cuba. Worried about U.S. efforts to overthrow Fidel Castro at the Bay of Pigs, the Russians pledged to support Cuba in the future. In October 1962, aerial photographs taken by a U.S. spy plane revealed that the Soviet Union had begun to place what Kennedy considered offensive nuclear missiles in Cuba. The presence of these missiles did not change the strategic balance, for the Soviets could still

"See how many are staying on our side."

Some residents of East Berlin wanted to leave, but the wall bisecting the city prevented their passage. This cartoon shows their inability, despite vigorous efforts, to get over the heavily fortified wall, while Khrushchev proclaims with a smile that they are happy to stay on the communist side.

One toy manufacturer used Kennedy's confrontation with Khrushchev to create a board game called "Bluff." It featured cartoon representations of both leaders on the lid of the box (with Kennedy in a rocking chair for his bad back), and promised players the chance to try to outwit their opponents.

wreak terrible havoc on U.S. targets from bases farther away. But their presence nevertheless demanded a response.

After the humiliation at the Bay of Pigs and his inability to do anything about the wall in Berlin, Kennedy was determined to win this confrontation with the Soviet Union. He convened the Executive Committee of the National Security Council to debate the various strategic alternatives. Some members wanted an air strike to knock out the missile sites. Others counseled a more restrained approach. In the end, the President went on nationwide television to tell the American people about the missiles and make a public demand for their removal. In the document excerpted here he declared that the United States would not shrink from the risk of nuclear war and announced that he was throwing a naval blockade around Cuba to prevent the Soviets from bringing in any more missiles. He was careful, however, to call the move a quarantine, for installing a blockade was an act of war.

Soviet ships continued to steam toward the blockade, and for two days the world stood at the brink of disaster. The tension broke only when Khrushchev called the Russian ships back. He then sent Kennedy a long letter pledging to remove the missiles if the United States would end the blockade and promise to stay out of Cuba. Then, in a second letter, he demanded that the United States remove its own missiles from Turkey (an action already ordered by Kennedy several months before). The United States responded affirmatively to the first letter but ignored the second. With that, the crisis came to an end.

Attorney General Robert F. Kennedy, the President's brother, resisted launching an air strike. Referring to the Japanese leader responsible for the attack on Pearl Harbor that drew the United States into World War II, he said over and over, "My brother is not going to be the Tojo of the 1960s."

The Cuban missile crisis was the most terrifying confrontation of the cold war. At that time the world was closer to nuclear war than ever before and felt itself lucky to have survived. In the immediate aftermath, Kennedy was first hailed as a hero who had stood firm, but later critics charged that what he liked to portray as his finest hour was in fact an excessive response that escalated the crisis.

One response to the crisis was renewed agitation to try to control nuclear arms. That effort led to the Limited Test Ban Treaty, banning atmospheric and underwater nuclear testing, signed in the summer of 1963 by the United States, the U.S.S.R., and Britain.

This Government, as promised, has maintained the closest surveillance of the Soviet military buildup on the island of Cuba. Within the past week, unmistakable evidence has established the fact that a series of offensive missile sites is now in preparation on that imprisoned land. The purpose of these bases can be none other than to provide a nuclear strike capability against the Western Hemisphere. . . .

The characteristics of these new missile sites indicate two distinct types of installations. Several of them include medium range ballistic missiles, capable of carrying a nuclear warhead for a distance of more than 1,000 nautical miles. Each of these missiles, in short, is capable of striking Washington, D.C., the Panama Canal, Cape Canaveral, Mexico City, or any other city in the southeastern part of the United States, in Central America, or in the Caribbean area.

Additional sites not yet completed appear to be designed for intermediate range ballistic missiles—capable of traveling more than twice as far—and thus capable of striking most of the major cities in the Western Hemisphere, ranging as far north as Hudson Bay, Canada, and as far south as Lima, Peru. In addition, jet bombers, capable of carrying nuclear weapons, are now being uncrated and assembled in Cuba, while the necessary air bases are being prepared.

This urgent transformation of Cuba into an important strategic base—by the presence of these large, long-range, and clearly offensive weapons of sudden mass destruction—constitutes an explicit threat to the peace and security of all the Americas. . .

Neither the United States of America nor the world community of nations can tolerate deliberate deception and offensive

The United States worried about Cuba's commitment to communism, especially since the island nation was so close to the United States. Posters in Cuba showing (from left to right) Karl Marx, co-author of the Communist Manifesto, *Vladimir Ilich Lenin, leader of the Bolshevik Revolution, and Fidel Castro, Cuban communist leader, made that commitment clear.*

According to Anatoly Dobrynin, who served for many years as Soviet ambassador to the United States, Khrushchev placed missiles in Cuba as "part of a broader geopolitical strategy to achieve greater parity with the United States that would be useful not only in the dispute over Berlin but in negotiations on other issues."

We're eyeball to eyeball, and I think the other fellow just blinked.

—Secretary of State Dean Rusk, expressing the relief of U.S. officials when missile-carrying Soviet ships heading toward the blockade line stopped and turned around

threats on the part of any nation, large or small. We no longer live in a world where only the actual firing of weapons represents a sufficient challenge to a nation's security to constitute maximum peril. Nuclear weapons are so destructive and ballistic missiles are so swift, that any substantially increased possibility of their use or any sudden change in their deployment may well be regarded as a definite threat to peace. . . .

Our policy has been one of patience and restraint, as befits a peaceful and powerful nation, which leads a worldwide alliance. We have been determined not to be diverted from our central concerns by mere irritants and fanatics. But now further action is required—and it is under way; and these actions may only be the beginning. We will not prematurely or unnecessarily risk the costs of worldwide nuclear war in which even the fruits of victory would be ashes in our mouth—but neither will we shrink from that risk at any time it must be faced.

Acting, therefore, in the defense of our own security and of the entire Western Hemisphere, . . . I have directed that the following *initial* steps be taken immediately:

First: To halt this offensive buildup, a strict quarantine on all offensive military equipment under shipment to Cuba is being initiated. . . .

Second: I have directed the continued and increased close surveillance of Cuba and its military buildup. . . .

Third: It shall be the policy of this Nation to regard any nuclear missile launched from Cuba against any nation in the Western Hemisphere as an attack by the Soviet Union on the United States, requiring a full retaliatory response upon the Soviet Union.

Fourth: As a necessary military precaution, I have reinforced our base at Guantanamo [in Cuba], evacuated today the dependents of our personnel there, and ordered additional military units to be on a standby alert basis.

Fifth: We are calling tonight for an immediate meeting of the Organ of Consultation under the Organization of American States, to consider this threat to hemispheric security. . .

Sixth: Under the Charter of the United Nations, we are asking tonight that an emergency meeting of the Security Council be convoked without delay to take action against this latest Soviet threat to world peace. . . .

Seventh and finally: I call upon Chairman Khrushchev to halt and eliminate this clandestine, reckless, and provocative threat to world peace and to stable relations between our two nations. I call upon him further to abandon this course of world domination, and

MRBM LAUNCH SITE 1
SAN CRISTOBAL, CUBA
23 OCTOBER 1962

MISSILE ERECTOR

CABLE

MISSILE SHELTER TENT

TRACKED PRIME MOVERS

FUEL TANK TRAILERS

OXIDIZER TANK TRAILERS

This arial photograph, taken at the start of the Cuban missile crisis, shows where the Soviet Union had placed medium range ballistic missiles in San Cristobal, Cuba.

to join in an historic effort to end the perilous arms race and to transform the history of man. . . .

My fellow citizens: let no one doubt that this is a difficult and dangerous effort on which we have set out. No one can foresee precisely what course it will take or what costs or casualties will be incurred. Many months of sacrifice and self-discipline lie ahead—months in which both our patience and our will will be tested—months in which many threats and denunciations will keep us aware of our dangers. But the greatest danger of all would be to do nothing.

The path we have chosen for the present is full of hazards, as all paths are—but it is the one most consistent with our character and courage as a nation and our commitments around the world. The cost of freedom is always high—but Americans have always paid it. And one path we shall never choose, and that is the path of surrender or submission.

Our goal is not the victory of might, but the vindication of right—not peace at the expense of freedom, but both peace *and* freedom, here in this hemisphere, and, we hope, around the world. God willing, that goal will be achieved.

Chapter Four: Picture Essay

The Atom Unleashed

The development of atomic weapons complicated the cold war. The new bombs dropped on the Japanese cities of Hiroshima and Nagasaki at the end of World War II inaugurated a nuclear arms race that threatened to devastate the globe. The postwar antagonism between the Soviet Union and the United States became increasingly serious as both nations stockpiled weapons capable of destroying millions of people and perhaps even wiping out the human race.

The Manhattan Project, which created the first atomic bomb, began in 1942. Its origins lay in a letter from Albert Einstein (see chapter 1) alerting President Franklin D. Roosevelt about the possibility of a new source of energy that might be harnessed into a weapon of war. Over the next three years, the developmental effort mobilized scientists in the largest project yet attempted to produce a bomb having an explosive power barely imaginable before.

By the summer of 1945, the United States was ready to test its new weapon. The atomic bomb was based on the process of fission, which required splitting the nuclei of atoms in an ongoing reaction capable of releasing an enormous explosive force. In a test at Alamogordo, in the New Mexico desert, scientists demonstrated that they had done their work well when the weapon's fireball broke the predawn darkness and made older bombs pale by comparison.

U.S. policy makers decided to use the new bomb to try to end World War II. An invasion of the Japanese home islands had already been planned, but it carried with it the possibility of large numbers of casualties. Officials debated about organizing a blockade or continuing with conventional bombing to try to force Japan to surrender, but they concluded that the atomic bomb had in fact been developed for wartime use and therefore decided to drop it on Japan.

The mushroom cloud from atomic explosions became the icon of the atomic age. The bomb dropped on Nagasaki on August 8, 1945, the second atomic bomb ever used, created a dense column of smoke that rose more than 60,000 feet into the air and was both fascinating and horrifying at the same time.

On August 6, 1945, an American bomber dropped an atomic bomb nicknamed "Little Boy" on Hiroshima. "My God," scribbled the copilot of the *Enola Gay*, the B-29 bomber that carried the bomb, as he watched it explode. The new weapon killed 70,000 people, injured 70,000 more, and reduced the city to rubble. Hiroshima after the blast looked similar to cities, such as Tokyo, destroyed by more conventional weapons, but devastation there had been caused by hundreds of bombs. Hiroshima was leveled by a single blast.

The physical destruction of the first atomic explosions was overwhelming, but the human devastation was even worse. People who survived the initial blast suffered from serious burns that all too often refused to heal. The light from the blast was so strong that it seared clothing patterns onto the victims' skin. Many of the wounded victims limped along for a few days but then died. Those who survived bore the scars of the bombing for the rest of their lives.

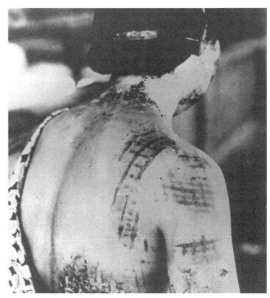

As the United States began to test new bombs, Americans became fascinated by the mushroom clouds they produced. The clouds were awesome, changing shape as they grew, as if transmuting into something altogether new. They also conjured up ominous associations. In Western culture, mushrooms were traditionally associated with dark, rotting places, as well as with poison and death, although they might also be identified with food, and hence with life. Sometimes the mushroom cloud became a symbol of force. A 1955 Atomic Energy Commission (AEC) film declared that "the towering cloud of the atomic age is a symbol of strength . . . for freedom loving peoples." This cloud from a test at the Bikini atoll in the Pacific Ocean in 1946 had particularly attractive symmetry.

While some Americans were worried by the atomic bombs, more were delighted by the new weapons that promised to bring the war to a speedy end. The early public reactions in the United States were often light-hearted. Hours after the announcement of the bomb being dropped on Hiroshima, the Washington Press Club developed an alcoholic drink called the Atomic Cocktail, made from a combination of Pernod and gin.

ANATOMIC BOMB
Starlet Linda Christians brings the new atomic age to Hollywood

The week that Japan surrendered, *Life* magazine ran a picture of starlet Linda Christians, dressed in a two-piece bathing suit, over the caption "Anatomic Bomb." It was a calculated attempt to liken the bomb's force to the actress's sex appeal as she launched her Hollywood career. Atomic terms soon found their way into the national vocabulary. Following a test at the Pacific Island of Bikini, a French fashion designer called a skimpy new women's bathing suit a bikini to call attention to its explosive promise.

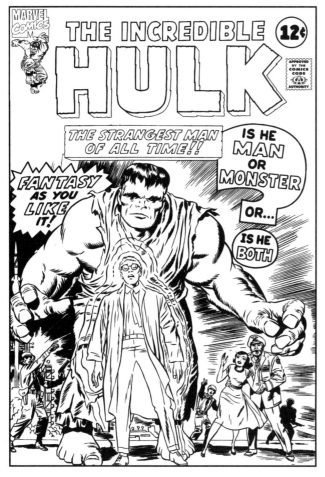

The world of popular culture also seized upon the consequences of radioactivity. In 1962, writer Stan Lee started a new comic-book series about Bruce Banner, a mild-mannered scientist accidentally exposed to radioactive gamma rays in testing a new bomb. Banner survived the blast but now had the ability to change into "The Hulk." "The Hulk" was a mutant, but he was not harmful or evil. He was, Lee felt, a Frankenstein's monster, with the old story simply updated: "Our hero would be a scientist, translated into a raging behemoth by a nuclear accident. And—since I was willing to borrow from Frankenstein, I decided I might as well borrow from Dr. Jekyll and Mr. Hyde as well—our protagonist would constantly change from his normal identity to his superhuman alter ego and back again."

Also in 1962, Stan Lee introduced another radioactive freak: Peter Parker, a high school student interested in atomic science. During a laboratory experiment, a spider absorbed a large amount of radioactivity and bit Parker, giving him incredible new powers that allowed him to become "Spider-Man." After the spider bite, Peter Parker asked, "What's **happening** to me? I feel—different! As though my entire body is charged with some sort of fantastic energy." As he discovered that he could scale walls in seconds and crush steel pipes with his bare hands, he realized, "It's the **spider**! It **has** to be! Somehow—in some miraculous way, his bite has transferred his own power—to **me**!"

In the 1950s, atomic weapons—which derived their force from splitting atoms apart—gave way to the far more powerful hydrogen weapons, which were based on an atomic fusion reaction that approximated what occurs on the surface of the sun. On March 1, 1954, in the Bravo test, the United States exploded its first operational hydrogen bomb, and it brought new problems. When winds blew radioactive ash onto the crew members of a Japanese fishing vessel, the crewmen soon began to suffer from radiation sickness. When one of them died of complications, the world became aware of the menace of fallout. The cartoonist Herblock (Herbert Block) pictured the ever-expanding danger from fallout.

Fallout soon became a household word. People worried about the lethal effects of radioactive debris being scattered around the globe by nuclear tests. In 1958, the Committee for Nuclear Information at Washington University in St. Louis collected tens of thousands of baby teeth and demonstrated how strontium-90—the most prevalent radioactive element—traveled up the food chain to end up in humans themselves. Fear of fallout created a groundswell of support for an end to nuclear testing. Pediatrician Benjamin Spock, the internationally known author of *Baby and Child Care*, spoke out on behalf of the National Committee for a Sane Nuclear Policy, better known simply as SANE. In a full-page 1962 newspaper advertisement, he appeared with a worried frown on his face, voicing his concern.

Dr. Spock is worried.

The lethal power of the atom convinced policy makers that they needed to find a way to protect their citizen populations. The solution they endorsed was a campaign for civil defense. One of the first initiatives they adopted was to persuade people to drop to the ground and try to safeguard themselves in the event of an attack. Millions of school children were taught to hide under their desks. Bert the Turtle was the hero of a campaign that unfolded in comic books and an animated film that taught people to "Duck and Cover."

When policy makers realized that the "Duck and Cover" campaign could not begin to protect people from an atomic blast, they proposed a program for evacuation instead. The Interstate Highway Act of 1956 justified a major road-building program by arguing that it would allow Americans to escape a nuclear attack. Meanwhile, some leaders wanted to provide various kinds of shelters as an alternative means of protection. When blast shelters proved to be too expensive, they opted for fallout shelters instead. The purpose of these shelters was to let survivors of an attack retreat underground and wait until the most dangerous radioactivity disappeared and it was safe to come out, presumably in a matter of weeks. Fallout shelters came in all shapes and sizes. This basement family fallout shelter included a 14-day supply of food and water, a battery-powered radio, auxiliary light sources, and first aid and sanitary supplies.

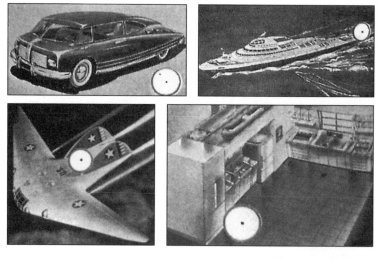

Fears of the atom were offset by hopes of a brave new world where atomic power could benefit the human race. The generation of nuclear power was one important possibility, and people spoke hopefully about power that would be "too cheap to meter." If heat from a controlled nuclear reaction could be used to drive a turbine, they argued, it should be possible to generate electricity and to power all kinds of vehicles and appliances with this new technology. Just weeks after the bombing of Hiroshima and Nagasaki, on August 20, 1945, *Newsweek* magazine pictured a car, a plane, an ocean liner, and a kitchen, all fueled by the atom.

Hopes for peaceful uses of atomic energy soared after World War II. The most popular promoter was cartoonist Walt Disney. His animated film *Our Friend the Atom* explored the scientific background of atomic energy, then described the architecture of the atom in terms that children could understand. For those who missed the movie, author Heinz Haber provided the same material in book form in 1956, with *The Walt Disney Story of Our Friend the Atom*. The first picture in the book was a mushroom cloud, symbolizing the violent and frightening side of atomic energy. The last picture, the city scene here, presented the hopeful possibilities of using atomic energy peacefully.

Nuclear power plants became a reality in the 1950s. The first facility, built at Shippingport, Pennsylvania, went on line in 1957, and many more followed. Occasional accidents proved worrisome, but a basic commitment to nuclear energy remained. Then came a dramatic accident at the Three Mile Island nuclear plant, pictured here, near Harrisburg, Pennsylvania, in March 1979. Part of the nuclear core became uncovered by its cooling water, some of it disintegrated, and the steam and water in the system became highly radioactive. The possibility that an explosion could release radioactivity into the atmosphere led thousands of area residents to flee. After 12 days the danger passed, but the plant remained shut down, a monument to a form of energy that had once seemed promising but now appeared more destructive than it was worth.

Fears of a cataclysmic nuclear war revived in the 1980s. As efforts to control arms faltered, more and more sophisticated nuclear weapons threatened to obliterate the human race. In 1982, a report by Congress's Office of Technology Assessment showed both the immediate and long-term effects of a nuclear war, with calculations of the damage done by different-sized bombs. Taking Detroit as one example, it provided a map showing regions that would be destroyed and areas that would be contaminated by fallout. The map conveyed the impression that this was a real U.S. city, inhabited by real American citizens, that could be wiped out in a nuclear war.

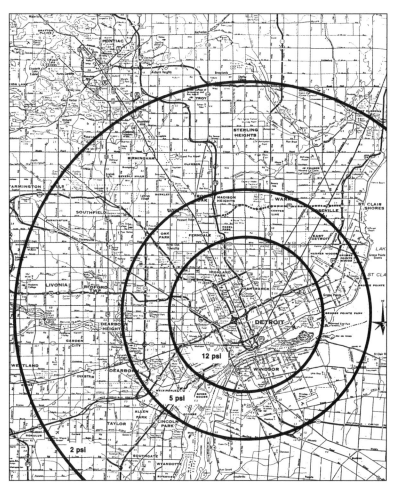

Chapter Five

Catastrophe in Vietnam

After World War II, the cold war commitments of the United States led it into a catastrophic war in Vietnam. Concerned about the spread of communism around the world, Americans became involved in a struggle in Indochina, in Southeast Asia, south of China. There for decades Vietnamese forces had sought to free the region from French colonial rule. For an America caught up in the cold war, any challenge to Western authority by elements sympathetic to communism became a cause for alarm.

The U.S. role developed by degrees. At first the United States did nothing more than provide financial aid to France, in return for French support of the U.S. policy of containing communism in Europe. Later, after France suffered a disastrous defeat in Vietnam in 1954 and withdrew from the country, the United States filled the void, taking responsibility for the military struggle against what it viewed as another incarnation of the communist menace. In the 1960s, U.S. involvement escalated until more than half a million American soldiers were fighting in a war that ravaged Vietnam but still seemed impossible to win.

The conflict in Vietnam, America's longest war, lasted for decades, from the very end of World War II all the way up to the final resolution in 1975. It was also the least successful cold war confrontation for the United States. In the end, after losing more than 58,000 soldiers and spending more than $150 billion, the United States was forced to withdraw its forces and accept a humiliating defeat. The communist triumph left a bitter taste after the long, laborious effort. Vietnam became a symbol of the turbulence of America in the 1960s and the fault lines that shifted the ground under American society.

The war in Vietnam was fought all over the country, in jungles and rice paddies as well as in cities. Here American marines move along rice paddy dikes in search of fleeing members of the communist Viet Cong.

Ho Chi Minh was the communist leader who fought for the independence of Vietnam against the French, then the Japanese, and finally the United States. Propaganda pictures often showed Ho Chi Minh with children to convey the impression that he was the father of his country.

As World War II wound down, William J. Donovan, director of the Office of Strategic Services, cited a statement by Vietnamese independence leaders: "Should the French attempt to return to Indo-China with the intention of governing the country, and to act once more as oppressors, the Indo-Chinese people are prepared to fight to the end against any such reoccupation."

French Colonial Rule

The roots of the war stretched far into the past. France had conquered Indochina—which includes present-day Vietnam, Thailand, Laos, and Cambodia—in the middle of the 19th century and had ruled as the dominant colonial power until Japan had moved into the region at the start of World War II. During the war, the Japanese permitted a French puppet government to remain in power, but France was discredited by the ease with which the Japanese had seized control. Meanwhile, Ho Chi Minh, an ardent Vietnamese nationalist and a communist organizer with ties to the Soviet Union, fought for the independence of his homeland. Ho had lived in France, worked as a revolutionary in Russia, China, Thailand, and Vietnam, and established the Indochinese Communist Party in 1930. In 1940 he returned to Vietnam and founded the Vietnamese independence movement known as the Vietminh.

Toward the end of World War II, the Japanese deposed the French government it had permitted to retain nominal power. Now the Vietminh waged a guerrilla war against the new colonial masters. When Japan surrendered to the Allied powers in August 1945, the Vietminh moved into government headquarters in Hanoi and on September 2, 1945, proclaimed the Democratic Republic of Vietnam. The new government's Declaration of Independence had an eerie similarity to its U.S. counterpart.

All men are created equal. They are endowed by their Creator with certain inalienable rights, among these are Life, Liberty and the pursuit of Happiness.

This immortal statement was made in the Declaration of Independence of the United States of America in 1776. In a broader sense, this means: All the peoples on the earth are equal from birth, all the peoples have a right to live, to be happy and free.

The Declaration of the French Revolution made in 1791 on the Rights of Man and the Citizen also states: "All men are born free and with equal rights, and must always remain free and have equal rights."

Those are undeniable truths.

Nevertheless, for more than eighty years, the French imperialists, abusing the standard of Liberty, Equality, and Fraternity, have violated our Fatherland and oppressed our fellow-citizens. They have acted contrary to the ideals of humanity and justice.

In the field of politics, they have deprived our people of every democratic liberty. . . .

In the field of economics, they have fleeced us to the backbone, impoverished our people and devastated our land. . . .

In the Autumn of 1940, when the Japanese fascists violated Indochina's territory to establish new bases in their fight against the Allies, the French imperialists went down on their bended knees and handed over our country to them.

Thus, from that date, our people were subjected to the double yoke of the French and the Japanese. . . .

After the Japanese had surrendered to the Allies, our whole people rose to regain our national sovereignty and to found the Democratic Republic of Viet Nam. . . .

The whole Vietnamese people, animated by a common purpose, are determined to fight to the bitter end against any attempt by the French colonialists to reconquer their country. . . .

A people who have courageously opposed French domination for more than eighty years, a people who have fought side by side with the Allies against the fascists during these last years, such a people must be free and independent.

For these reasons we, members of the Provisional Government of the Democratic Republic of Viet Nam, solemnly declare to the world that Viet Nam has the right to be a free and independent country—and in fact it is so already. The entire Vietnamese people are determined to mobilize all their physical and mental strength, to sacrifice their lives and property in order to safeguard their independence and liberty.

The U.S. response to the Vietnamese declaration of independence was based on discussions during the war about what to do about colonialism in the postwar years. President Franklin D. Roosevelt recognized the forces undermining colonialism worldwide and understood the need to identify with the budding nationalist movements. He argued in favor of a program of trusteeship by the newly formed United Nations whereby colonies would receive assistance in making a gradual transition to independence. He was particularly intent on taking such an approach in Indochina, for he felt that the French had treated the region badly and he wanted to avoid a return by France. In early 1944, Roosevelt made his views clear to Cordell Hull, his secretary of state, when he described a conversation with Lord Halifax, a British diplomat.

After Ho Chi Minh issued his proclamation to a crowd of several hundred thousand people, Vo Nguyen Giap, a former teacher and now military leader, declared, "As regards foreign relations, our public opinion pays very much attention to the Allied missions in Hanoi because everyone is anxious to know the result of the foreign negotiations of the government." He spoke of "particularly intimate relations" with the Americans, "which it is a pleasant duty to dwell upon."

I've met many people in the course of my political career, but Ho Chi Minh impressed me in a very special way. Religious people used to talk about the holy apostles. Well, by the way he lived and by the way he impressed other people, Ho Chi Minh was like one of those "holy apostles." He was an apostle of the Revolution.

I'll never forget the look in his eye, the way his gaze shone with a special kind of sincerity and purity. It was the sincerity of an incorruptible Communist and the purity of a man devoted in principle and in practice to the cause.

—Nikita S. Khrushchev, Soviet leader at the time of the Hungarian uprising

British Prime Minister Winston Churchill opposed Roosevelt's position on trusteeship in general, for he was worried about the erosion of Britain's colonial influence. "Let me . . . make this clear, in case there should be any mistake about it in any quarter," he proclaimed in 1942. "I have not become the King's First Minister in order to preside over the liquidation of the British Empire."

I saw Halifax last week and told him quite frankly that it was perfectly true that I had, for over a year, expressed the opinion that Indo-China should not go back to France but that it should be administered by an international trusteeship. France has had the country—thirty million inhabitants—for nearly one hundred years, and the people are worse off than they were at the beginning. . . .

Each case must, of course, stand on its own feet, but the case of Indo-China is perfectly clear. France has milked it for one hundred years. The people of Indo-China are entitled to something better than that.

War in Indochina

When Harry S. Truman became President following Roosevelt's death in April 1945, U.S. policy became even more favorable toward France. Despite a series of communications from Ho Chi Minh describing devastating conditions, invoking the principles of self-determination outlined in various international agreements like the Charter of the United Nations, and asking for recognition of independence, or, at the very least, trusteeship under the UN, the United States refused to act. By the summer of 1945, the Truman administration was giving French leader Charles de Gaulle assurances that it would not stop France from reestablishing French sovereignty in Indochina. But the Vietnamese were determined to resist the return of the French and war broke out.

Initially, the State Department questioned whether France understood the intensity of Vietnam's nationalism and had the capacity to squelch the revolution. By 1947, however, the United States found that it needed France's help to contain communism in Europe, so it gave France substantial amounts of economic aid, which enabled the French to shift their own resources to Vietnam. A telegram from Secretary of State George C. Marshall to the U.S. Embassy in France in early 1947 summarized U.S. concerns and conclusions.

In mid-1945, the Truman administration concluded that the United States "had no interest" in "championing schemes of international trusteeship" that would undermine the "European states whose help we need to balance Soviet power in Europe."

There is reason for increasing concern over situation as it is developing in Indochina. . . . We have only very friendliest feelings toward France and we are anxious in every way we can to support France in her fight to regain her economic, political, and military strength and to restore herself as in fact one of major powers of the world. In spite any misunderstanding which might have arisen in minds [of] French in regard to our position concerning

VIỆT-NAM DÂN CHỦ CỘNG HÒA

CHÍNH PHỦ LÂM THỜI

BO NGOAI GIAO
*

HANOI FEBRUARY 28 1946

TELEGRAM   MAR 11 RECD

PRESIDENT HOCHIMINH VIETNAM DEMOCRATIC REPUBLIC HANOI

TO THE PRESIDENT OF THE UNITED STATES OF AMERICA WASHINGTON D.C.

ON BEHALF OF VIETNAM GOVERNMENT AND PEOPLE I BEG TO INFORM YOU

THAT IN COURSE OF CONVERSATIONS BETWEEN VIETNAM GOVERNMENT AND FRENCH

REPRESENTATIVES THE LATTER REQUIRE THE SECESSION OF COCHINCHINA AND THE

RETURN OF FRENCH TROOPS IN HANOI STOP MEANWHILE FRENCH POPULATION AND

TROOPS ARE MAKING ACTIVE PREPARATIONS FOR A COUP DE MAIN IN HANOI AND

FOR MILITARY AGGRESSION STOP I THEREFORE MOST EARNESTLY APPEAL TO YOU

PERSONALLY AND TO THE AMERICAN PEOPLE TO INTERFERE URGENTLY IN SUPPORT

OF OUR INDEPENDENCE AND HELP MAKING THE NEGOTIATIONS MORE IN KEEPING WITH

THE PRINCIPLES OF THE ATLANTIC AND SAN FRANCISCO CHARTERS

RESPECTFULLY

HOCHIMINH

As French rule returned to Vietnam at the end of World War II, Ho Chi Minh and other Vietnamese nationalists appealed to the United States for support for their independence movement. In this telegram, Ho Chi Minh cited the democratic principles for which World War II had been fought.

Indochina they must appreciate that we have fully recognized France's sovereign position in that area and we do not wish to have it appear that we are in any way endeavoring [to] undermine that position, and French should know it is our desire to be helpful and we stand ready [to] assist [in] any appropriate way we can to find solution for Indochinese problem. At same time we cannot shut our eyes to fact that there are two sides [to] this problem and that our reports indicate both a lack [of] French understanding of other side . . . and continued existence [of] dangerously outmoded colonial outlook and methods in area. Furthermore, there is no escape from fact that trend of times is to effect that colonial empires in XIX Century sense are rapidly becoming thing of past. . . . On other hand we do not lose sight [of] fact that Ho Chi Minh has direct Communist connections and it should be obvious that we are not interested in seeing colonial empire administrations supplanted by philosophy and political organization emanating from and controlled by Kremlin.

By 1948, the United States was still caught in the middle between wanting to acknowledge Vietnamese nationalism and maintain good relations with its traditional French ally. A State Department policy statement that year declared, "Our greatest difficulty in talking with the French and in stressing what should and what should not be done has been our inability to suggest any practicable solution of the Indochina problem, as we are all too well aware of the unpleasant fact that Communist Ho Chi Minh is the strongest and perhaps the ablest figure in Indochina and that any suggested solution which excludes him is an expedient of uncertain outcome."

The U.S. should not be self-duped into believing the possibility of partial involvement—such as "Naval and Air units only." One cannot go over Niagara Falls in a barrel only slightly.

—Vice Admiral A. C. Davis, voicing the reluctance of U.S. military officials to send American forces to Indochina

By the end of 1949, the United States was ready to make a far stronger commitment to supporting the French in Vietnam. American support for the French effort increased until by 1952 the United States was paying about one-third of France's cost of the war. Despite that assistance, the French were still having a hard time and wanted even more help. When Dwight D. Eisenhower succeeded Harry Truman as President in 1953, his new Republican administration accepted the basic outlines of the existing Indochina policy. Eisenhower and Secretary of State John Foster Dulles believed that Ho Chi Minh was an instrument of international communism and agreed that the fall of Indochina would have serious consequences for the United States. But their commitment to cutting defense spending made them reluctant to use American troops and they therefore insisted that the French continue to fight their own fight in Indochina and bear the burden of the war.

By early 1954 the French were in serious trouble in Indochina. Defending a garrison in the remote northwestern village of Dien Bien Phu, the French found themselves surrounded by troops led by General Giap, commander of the Vietnamese forces. Giap slowly but surely tightened the noose. Although French and American experts had argued that it would be impossible to move artillery up to the high ground around the garrison, "human ant-hills" of Vietminh forces carried disassembled weapons up piece by piece, then reassembled them at the top. Then they knocked out

The climactic battle in France's war against Vietnam came at Dien Bien Phu in 1954. At first French paratroopers managed to hold their own, but in the end they were unable to lift the siege of the garrison other French forces were trying to defend.

the airfield, eliminating the possibility of bringing in reinforcements.

The Eisenhower administration debated what to do. Reluctant to act unilaterally, Ike knew he needed the support of Congress but also wanted further assurances about French intentions. In his memoirs he observed that

Congressional support would be contingent upon meeting three conditions:

(1) United States intervention must be part of a coalition to include the other free nations of Southeast Asia, the Philippines, and the British Commonwealth.

(2) The French must agree to accelerate their independence program for the Associated States [of Indochina] so there could be no interpretation that United States assistance meant support of French colonialism.

(3) The French must agree not to pull their forces out of the war if we put our forces in.

The Geneva Conference

With no assistance forthcoming, Dien Bien Phu was doomed. After 56 days of shelling, the French surrendered the fortress on May 7, 1954. Earlier, France had agreed to place Indochina on the agenda of an international conference on Far Eastern problems to be held in Geneva, Switzerland. As Dien Bien Phu fell, the Indochina part of the discussion was just about to begin. The United States participated reluctantly at the Geneva Conference, with Secretary of State Dulles appearing only briefly, for the Chinese were present and the United States still refused to recognize the communist government. But the Russians and Chinese pressed for a settlement and got the victorious Vietminh to agree to a temporary partition of Vietnam at the 17th parallel following a cease-fire. The Final Declaration of the Geneva Conference recorded the agreement.

Final declaration, dated the 21st July, 1954, of the Geneva Conference on the problem of restoring peace in Indo-China, in which the representatives of Cambodia, the Democratic Republic of Viet-Nam, France, Laos, the People's Republic of China, the State of Viet-Nam, the Union of Soviet Socialist Republics, the United Kingdom, and the United States of America took part.

I am frankly of the belief that no amount of American military assistance in Indochina can conquer an enemy which is everywhere and at the same time nowhere, "an enemy of the people" which has the sympathy and covert support of the people.

—Democratic Senator John F. Kennedy, speaking out against U.S. intervention in Indochina, 1954

Secretary of State Dulles was clearly uncomfortable in the brief time he was at the Geneva Conference, behaving, according to one biographer, "with the pinched distaste of a puritan in a house of ill repute."

As discussions took place at the Geneva Conference, Ho Chi Minh's troops gained control of Vietnam north of the 17th parallel. Surrounded by cheering civilians, they entered the city of Hanoi, which had earlier been held by the French.

As the Geneva Conference continued, Dulles told congressional leaders that any agreement would be "something we would have to gag about," but still said that the United States might be able to "salvage something" in Southeast Asia "free of the taint of French colonialism." The reason for his optimism was that the United States had decided to take over responsibility for defending Indochina, particularly the part of Vietnam south of the partition line.

(1) The Conference takes note of the agreements ending hostilities in Cambodia, Laos and Viet-Nam and organizing international control and the supervision of the execution of the provisions of these agreements. . . .

(4) The Conference takes note of the clauses in the agreement on the cessation of hostilities in Viet-Nam prohibiting the introduction into Viet-Nam of foreign troops and military personnel as well as of all kinds of arms and munitions. . . .

(6) The Conference recognizes that the essential purpose of the agreement relating to Viet-Nam is to settle military questions with a view to ending hostilities and that the military demarcation line is provisional and should not in any way be interpreted as constituting a political or territorial boundary. . . .

(7) The Conference declares that, so far as Viet-Nam is concerned, the settlement of political problems, affected on the basis of respect for the principles of independence, unity and territorial integrity, shall permit the Viet-Namese people to enjoy the fundamental freedoms, guaranteed by democratic institutions established as a result of free general elections by secret ballot. In order to ensure that sufficient progress in the restoration of peace has been made, and that all the necessary conditions obtain for free expression of the national will, general elections shall be held in July 1956, under the supervision of an international commission. . . .

(10) The Conference takes note of the declaration of the Government of the French Republic to the effect that it is ready to

withdraw its troops from the territory of Cambodia, Laos, and Viet-Nam, at the requests of the Governments concerned. . . .

Nation Building in Vietnam

The United States quickly embarked on what it regarded as an experiment in nation-building. It wanted to create a free nation in the southern part of Vietnam—below the partition line—that would serve as a bulwark against communist expansion and as an example of democracy in Asia. France had finally granted independence to the region, but Ho Chi Minh controlled the territory in the north of Vietnam, while the Emperor Bao Dai, whom the French had installed as a figurehead ruler after their return to Indochina, still remained in power in the south. Bao Dai had been at best an ineffectual monarch.

American policy makers, looking for other alternatives, decided to work with Ngo Dinh Diem, a Vietnamese nationalist who had served in the colonial bureaucracy in the past. Diem was a fervent anticommunist who spoke out zealously in favor of Vietnamese independence during a period of self-imposed exile in the United States. His appeals for the creation of a free, noncommunist Vietnam brought him to the attention of American leaders who helped arrange his return to his country.

Diem turned out to be a rigid, autocratic leader. Aloof and introspective, he wholly lacked Ho Chi Minh's charismatic appeal. But the United States was determined to work with him, as President Eisenhower promised in a letter to him in the fall of 1954.

I have been following with great interest the course of developments in Vietnam, particularly since the conclusion of the conference at Geneva. The implications of the agreement concerning Vietnam have caused grave concern regarding the future of a country temporarily divided by an artificial military grouping, weakened by a long and exhausting war and faced with enemies without and by their subversive collaborators within. . . .

We have been exploring ways and means to permit our aid to Vietnam to be more effective and to make a greater contribution to the welfare and stability of the Government of Vietnam. I am, accordingly, instructing the American Ambassador to Vietnam to examine with you in your capacity as Chief of Government, how

As he was deciding in 1954 that the United States would take over the responsibility of supporting and defending Vietnam, President Eisenhower remarked, "We must work with these people, and then they themselves will soon find out that we are their friends and that they can't live without us."

Bao Dai, shown here with his wife, was the emperor the French had installed as a figurehead as they sought to reestablish their control. He had power in the south after France left Vietnam, but then lost a referendum to Ngo Dinh Diem, the leader brought back to govern South Vietnam by the United States, in 1955.

中国七亿人民是越南人民的坚强后盾

ZHONG GUO QI YI REN MIN SHI YUE NAN REN MIN DE JIAN QIANG HOU DUN

The United States worried about Chinese support for the communists in the war in Vietnam. This Chinese poster, showing worker, peasant, and soldier with raised fists in front of a crowd, contained the caption: "Seven hundred million people of China are the powerful backup force of the South Vietnamese people."

an intelligent program of American aid given directly to your Government can serve to assist Vietnam in its present hour of trial, provided that your Government is prepared to give assurances as to the standards of performance it would be able to maintain in the event such aid were supplied.

The purpose of this offer is to assist the Government of Vietnam in developing and maintaining a strong, viable state, capable of resisting attempted subversion or aggression through military means. The Government of the United States expects that this aid will be met by performance on the part of the Government of Vietnam in undertaking needed reforms. It hopes that such aid, combined with your own continuing efforts, will contribute effectively toward an independent Vietnam endowed with a strong government. Such a government would, I hope, be so responsive to the nationalist aspirations of its people, so enlightened in purpose and effective in performance, that it will be respected both at home and abroad and discourage any who might wish to impose a foreign ideology on your free people.

Over the next two years, Diem consolidated his power. Although he alienated some Vietnamese, he maintained his strong U.S. support. In 1955 he defeated Bao Dai in a referendum and now had total control over the government of South Vietnam, as his segment of the country came to be called. Though he paid lip service to democracy, he was an authoritarian ruler who tolerated no dissent. The promised elections to unify the two halves of the country never occurred. But U.S. aid continued to arrive, with Vietnam soon ranking fifth in the world in terms of assistance received. By the end of the 1950s, there were more than 1,500 Americans in Vietnam, 685 of them military advisors rather than active soldiers. Most Americans accepted the need to support this faraway country and applauded the policy of the United States. Senator John F. Kennedy summarized the prevailing view in a speech in mid-1956.

. . . Let us briefly consider exactly what is "America's Stake in Vietnam":

(1) *First*, Vietnam represents the cornerstone of the Free World in Southeast Asia, the keystone to the arch, the finger in the dike. Burma, Thailand, India, Japan, the Philippines and obviously Laos and Cambodia are among those whose security would be threatened if the Red Tide of Communism overflowed into Vietnam. . . .

Moreover, the independence of Free Vietnam is crucial to the free world in fields other than the military. Her economy is essential to the economy of all of Southeast Asia; and her political liberty is an inspiration to those seeking to obtain or maintain their liberty in all parts of Asia—and indeed the world. The fundamental tenets of this nation's foreign policy, in short, depend in considerable measure upon a strong and free Vietnamese nation.

(2) *Secondly*, Vietnam represents a proving ground of democracy in Asia. However we may choose to ignore it or deprecate it, the rising prestige and influence of Communist China in Asia are unchallengeable facts. Vietnam represents the alternative to Communist dictatorship. . . . The United States is directly responsible for this experiment—it is playing an important role in the laboratory where it is being conducted. We cannot afford to permit that experiment to fail.

(3) *Third* and in somewhat similar fashion, Vietnam represents a test of American responsibility and determination in Asia. If we are not the parents of little Vietnam, then surely we are the godparents. We presided at its birth, we gave assistance to its life, we have helped to shape its future. As French influence in the political, economic and military spheres has declined in Vietnam, American influence has steadily grown. This is our offspring—we cannot abandon it, we cannot ignore its needs. And if it falls victim to any of the perils that threaten its existence—Communism, political anarchy, poverty and the rest—then the United States, with some justification, will be held responsible; and our prestige in Asia will sink to a new low.

(4) *Fourth* and finally, America's stake in Vietnam, in her strength and in her security, is a very selfish one—for it can be measured, in the last analysis, in terms of American lives and American dollars . . . . Military weakness, political instability or economic failure in the new state of Vietnam could change almost overnight the apparent security which has increasingly characterized that area under the leadership of Premier Diem. And the key position of Vietnam in Southeast Asia . . . makes inevitable the involvement of this nation's security in any new outbreak of trouble. . . .

Ngo Dinh Diem, installed by the United States as the leader of South Vietnam after the French departure, established an iron-handed control over his country. Lyndon Johnson spoke with exaggeration in declaring on one occasion that Diem was "the Winston Churchill of Southeast Asia." Here he casts his ballot in April 1961 in an election that gave him a second five-year term.

For all of the U.S. aid it received, Vietnam remained, in the words of Milton Taylor, an American who served as a taxation advisor to the South Vietnamese government in 1959–1960, "the prototype of the dependent economy, its level of national income as dependent on outside forces as was the case when the country was a French colony. . . . American aid has built a castle on sand."

When Lyndon Johnson returned home from South Vietnam, he reported that time was running out and declared of Vietnam and a number of other countries that "the basic decision in Southeast Asia is here. We must decide whether to help these countries to the best of our ability or throw in the towel in the area and pull back our defenses to San Francisco and a 'Fortress America' concept."

The United States struggled to make the policy of containment—represented in this cartoon by the Great Wall of China—work successfully in Southeast Asia. But just as the wall had cracks in it, so the policy had problems, particularly after the partition of Vietnam at the Geneva Conference.

ANACHRONISM

Soon after becoming President in early 1961, John F. Kennedy received a report indicating that despite seven years of military, political, and economic assistance, the communists were gaining strength in Vietnam. In previous years, revolutionary forces attempting to overthrow the Diem government had formed the National Liberation Front (NLF), with the Viet Cong (VC) as its military arm. The Viet Cong and NLF were receiving assistance in their guerrilla war in the south from Ho Chi Minh and North Vietnam. Something needed to be done.

Kennedy dispatched Vice President Lyndon B. Johnson to South Vietnam to survey the situation and recommend a course of action. Meanwhile, he decided to expand U.S. aid programs and to increase economic and military support. He sent over 400 Special Forces troops, known as Green Berets, to engage in covert warfare and introduced regular forces as well. At the end of 1961, he wrote to President Diem, responding to a letter Diem had written to Kennedy, notifying the South Vietnamese leader of the expanded American commitment.

I have received your recent letter in which you described so cogently the dangerous condition caused by North Viet-Nam's efforts to take over your country. The situation in your embattled country is well known to me and to the American people. We have been deeply disturbed by the assault on your country. Our indignation has mounted as the deliberate savagery of the Communist program of assassination, kidnapping, and wanton violence became clear.

Your letter underlines what our own information has convincingly shown—that the campaign of force and terror now being waged against your people and your Government is supported and directed from the outside by the authorities at Hanoi. They have thus violated the provisions of the Geneva Accords designed to ensure peace in Viet-Nam and to which they bound themselves in 1954.

At that time, the United States, although not a party to the Accords, declared that it "would view any renewal of the aggression in violation of the agreements with grave concern and as seriously threatening international peace and security." We continue to maintain that view.

In accordance with that declaration, and in response to your request, we are prepared to help the Republic of Viet-Nam to protect its people and to preserve its independence. We shall promptly increase our assistance to your defense effort as well as help relieve the destruction of the floods which you describe. I have already given the orders to get these programs underway.

The United States, like the Republic of Viet-Nam, remains devoted to the cause of peace and our primary purpose is to help your people maintain their independence. If the Communist authorities in North Vietnam will stop their campaign to destroy the Republic of Viet-Nam, the measures we are taking to assist your defense efforts will no longer be necessary. We shall seek to persuade the Communists to give up their attempts of force and subversion. In any case, we are confident the Vietnamese people will preserve their independence and gain the peace and prosperity for which they have fought so hard and so long.

President Kennedy increased the number of Americans in Vietnam until there were about 25,000 by the end of 1963, with more than 16,000 of them soldiers, and the rest advisors. Yet the war was still not going well. Tension mounted as Diem became more authoritarian and tried to suppress political opponents. A Catholic himself, he miscalculated when he tried to silence Buddhist critics. In mid-1963, an aged Buddhist priest sat cross-legged in the street in downtown Saigon, doused himself with gasoline, and calmly lit a match. The blaze that killed him was captured in a photograph seen worldwide.

Photographs of Buddhist priests burning themselves to death in protest against the restrictions of the Diem regime appeared in newspapers around the world and horrified viewers. The pictures made it clear that Diem had lost the support of the Vietnamese people.

As more Buddhists incinerated themselves, Kennedy knew he had a problem. Initially, he reaffirmed U.S. support for Diem, but when word reached Washington that a group of South Vietnamese generals was ready to move against his government, U.S. officials, including the President, cabled Ambassador Henry Cabot Lodge instructing him to pass on the word that the United States was prepared to consider alternatives to Diem. One attack by the generals was called off, but then in early November 1963 South Vietnamese officers seized key military and communications installations and demanded Diem's resignation. When he refused and tried to escape, he and his brother were brutally murdered. Kennedy, though prepared for a change of government, was deeply troubled by the assassinations, which he had not expected.

By the end of the month, Kennedy himself was dead, the victim of an assassin's attack. When Vice President Lyndon B. Johnson assumed the Presidency, he received Ambassador Lodge, who had already been en route from Vietnam to brief Kennedy. After listening to Lodge, Johnson made a commitment to do whatever was necessary to defeat the communists and win the war.

Lyndon Johnson took a very personal interest in the war, even to the extent of choosing targets for American bombs. He remained in close touch with the Joint Chiefs of Staff, shown here meeting with him at his ranch in Texas, so that he could be involved in all military decisions.

But as he consolidated his own power, then ran for the Presidency in his own right in 1964, Johnson posed as a man of peace. He branded Republican candidate Barry Goldwater a warmonger, a man whose outspoken support for victory in Vietnam could lead to a much larger conflict. All the while, however, the Johnson administration was planning for war. In August 1964, Johnson responded to an alleged attack on U.S. destroyers in international waters of the Gulf of Tonkin, 30 miles from North Vietnam, by demanding and receiving from Congress a resolution authorizing any necessary retaliation. Passed by a unanimous vote in the House of Representatives and by a margin of 88 to 2 in the Senate, it authorized the President to take "all necessary measures to repel any armed attacks against the forces of the United States and to prevent further aggression." Johnson, pleased with the all-encompassing Gulf of Tonkin Resolution, remarked that it was "like Grandma's nightshirt—it covered everything." Only later did it become clear that the U.S. ships had intruded into North Vietnamese waters by assisting South Vietnamese in carrying out commando raids. In February 1965, after the U.S. election, Johnson retaliated for an attack on a U.S. base in Vietnam by ordering a massive bombing campaign of North Vietnam. Several months later, in an address at Johns Hopkins University, he outlined the U.S. position in the widening war.

Tonight, Americans and Asians are dying for a world where each people may choose its own path to change. This is the principle for which our ancestors fought in the valleys of Pennsylvania. It is a principle for which our sons fight tonight in the jungles of Viet-Nam.

Viet-Nam is far away from this quiet campus. We have no territory there, nor do we seek any. The war is dirty and brutal and difficult. And some 400 young men, born into an America that is bursting with opportunity and promise, have ended their lives on Viet-Nam's steaming soil.

Why must we take this painful road? Why must this nation hazard its ease, its interest, and its power for the sake of a people so far away?

We fight because we must fight if we are to live in a world where every country can shape its own destiny, and only in such a world will our own freedom be finally secure. . . .

Why are we in South Vietnam?

I am not going to lose Vietnam. I am not going to be the President who saw Southeast Asia go the way China went.
—President Johnson, to Ambassador Henry Cabot Lodge, shortly after taking office in 1963

That was the dry season when the sun burned harshly, the wind blew fiercely, and the enemy sent napalm spraying through the jungle and a sea of fire enveloped them, spreading like the fires of hell. Troops in the fragmented companies tried to regroup, only to be blown out of their shelters again as they went mad, became disoriented and threw themselves into nets of bullets, dying in the flaming inferno. Above them the helicopters flew at tree-top height and shot them almost one by one, the blood spreading out, spraying from their backs, flowing like red mud.

—Bao Ninh, North Vietnamese writer, *The Sorrow of War: A Novel*, 1993

A No-Win Situation

Despite his commitment to support the war as vigorously as he could, Johnson became frustrated at its impact on his reform program, the Great Society, back home. Describing his feelings about the escalation in early 1965, he told historian Doris Kearns: "I knew from the start that I was bound to be crucified either way I moved. If I left the woman I really loved—the Great Society—in order to get involved with that bitch of a war on the other side of the world, then I would lose everything at home. All my programs. All my hopes to feed the hungry and shelter the homeless. All my dreams to provide education and medical care to the browns and the blacks and the lame and the poor. But if I left that war and let the Communists take over South Vietnam, then I would be seen as a coward and my nation would be seen as an appeaser and we would both find it impossible to accomplish anything for anybody anywhere on the entire globe."

Because it was not always clear who had won a battle, the military began to define victory in terms of body counts. If there were more Viet Cong than American corpses, a skirmish was declared a triumph for the United States. Under pressure from their commanders to produce enemy corpses, soldiers often counted civilians as Viet Cong. The rule of thumb was, "If it's dead and Vietnamese, it's VC."

We are there because we have a promise to keep. Since 1954 every American President has offered support to the people of South Viet-Nam. We have helped to build, and we have helped to defend. Thus, over many years, we have made a national pledge to help South Viet-Nam defend its independence.

And I intend to keep that promise.

To dishonor that pledge, to abandon this small and brave nation to its enemies, and to the terror that must follow, would be an unforgivable wrong.

We are also there to strengthen world order. Around the globe, from Berlin to Thailand, are people whose well-being rests in part on the belief that they can count on us if they are attacked. To leave Viet-Nam to its fate would shake the confidence of all these people in the value of an American commitment and in the value of America's word. The result would be increased unrest and instability, and even wider war.

We are also there because there are great stakes in the balance. Let no one think for a moment that retreat from Viet-Nam would bring an end to conflict. The battle would be renewed in one country and then in another. The central lesson of our time is that the appetite of aggression is never satisfied. To withdraw from one battlefield means only to prepare for the next. We must say in Southeast Asia—as we did in Europe—in the words of the Bible: "Hitherto shalt thou come, but no further.". . .

Horrors of War

Escalation became the order of the day in Vietnam. The number of U.S. forces increased dramatically, to 184,000 in 1965, 385,000 in 1966, 485,000 in 1967, and 543,000 in 1968. Yet the soldiers had a difficult time in the war. It was hard to tell North Vietnamese from South Vietnamese, or Viet Cong from supporters of the anticommunist government supported by the United States. Combat troops, often unable to find the enemy, were frustrated at skirmishes that did not seem to bring any visible results. As one soldier, interviewed by author Mark Baker, observed:

In a fire fight you got twenty guys over there shooting at you and you got twenty or thirty guys over here, shooting back at them. We'll call in artillery fire. They're calling in mortar fire. Somebody decides, "Okay, I've had enough." Then that's over. But there was no ground taken. Nobody won anything or moved their lines.

Sometimes the waiting was even worse. But then, all of a sudden, a soldier found himself at risk from a sniper or a mine. The soldier continued:

There was a lot of tedious nonsense you had to put up with around there. There was a knack to doing everything at a slow pace. You had to learn patience. You wind up learning.

Bouncing Betty was bad. A Bouncing Betty is a land mine. You step on a spring here and Bouncing Betty comes up somewhere else over there. She would jump up about four or five feet and then she blows, spraying down and out. When she goes off, about the only thing you can do is try to get under it. Dive, hit the ground and lie flat as tight as you can. If you're close enough, it will miss you or you may just get a little piece of shrapnel here or there, something you could live with. Problem is, it's always someone else who sets Betty off on you. You can be as careful as you want, but if some asshole goes skipping down the trail, he may pop Bouncing Betty on you.

There were a lot of those punji sticks, swing limbs and little spring-detonated bombs in old C-ration cans. That's why I didn't like that area. I could deal with a man. That meant my talent against his for survival, but how do you deal with him when he ain't even there. . . .

Sometimes soldiers simply went berserk. In 1968, a U.S. infantry company was sent by helicopter to clear out the small village of My Lai in South Vietnam, said to be harboring 250 members of the Viet Cong. Charlie Company, whose First Platoon was commanded by Lieutenant William Calley, Jr., had already taken heavy combat losses and the men were edgy. Instead of Vietnamese troops, they found women, children, and old men. Perhaps hardened by the physical destruction and loss of life they had already encountered, or unsure how to distinguish between soldiers and civilians in a guerrilla war, the U.S. forces lost control and mowed down several hundred Vietnamese civilians in cold blood. Paul Meadlo, one of the participants, described the event in an interview:

Q: How many people did you round up?

A: Well, there was about 40–45 people that we gathered in the center of the village. And we placed them in there, and it was like a little island, right there in the center of the village, I'd say. And—

Q: What kind of people—men, women, children?

The war was difficult for American forces, who were fighting not to control territory but to contain the communist population. Here an American marine guards a member of the Viet Cong as they move toward a collection point for captured enemy troops.

Injured soldiers often came home bitter. Ron Kovic, paralyzed by a bullet that shattered his spinal cord, summed up the frustration many felt in a poem about the war:

I am the living death
the memorial day on wheels
I am your yankee doodle dandy
your john wayne come home
your fourth of July firecracker
exploding in the grave.

*Hey, Hey, LBJ, How many
kids did you kill today?*
          —Antiwar slogan

A: Men, women, children.

Q: Babies?

A: Babies. And we all huddled them up. We made them squat down, and Lieutenant Calley came over and said you know what to do with them, don't you. And I said Yes. So I took it for granted that he just wanted us to watch them. And he left, and came back about 10 or 15 minutes later, and said, how come you ain't killed them yet? And I told him that I didn't think you wanted us to kill them, that you just wanted us to guard them. He said, no, I want them dead. So——

Q: He told this to all of you, or to you particularly?

A: Well, I was facing him. So, but, the other three, four guys heard it and so he stepped back about 10, 15 feet, and he started shooting them. And he told me to start shooting. So I poured about four clips into the group.

Q: You fired four clips from your. . .

A: M-16.

Q: And that's about—how many clips—I mean how many——

A: I carried seventeen rounds to each clip.

Q: So you fired something like 67 shots——

*As the war involved increasing
numbers of U.S. troops, American
students began demonstrating
against the war. Their actions
in marches and rallies helped to
persuade the U.S. government to
withdraw from Vietnam.*

A: Right.

Q: And you killed how many? At that time?

A: Well, I fired them on automatic, so you can't—you just spray the area on them and so you can't know how many you killed 'cause they were going fast. So I might have killed ten or fifteen of them.

Q: Men, women and children?

A: Men, women and children.

Q: And babies?

A: And babies.

Q: Okay, then what?

A: So we started to gather them up, more people, and we had about seven or eight people, that we was gonna put into the hootch, and we dropped a hand grenade in there with them. . . .

Q: Why did you do it?

A: Why did I do it? Because I felt like I was ordered to do it, and it seemed like that, at the time I felt like I was doing the right thing, because like I said I lost buddies. I lost a damn good buddy, Bobby Wilson, and it was on my conscience. So after I done it, I felt good, but later on that day, it was getting to me. . . .

Q: Did you ever dream about all of this? . . .

A: Yes I did. . . and I still dream about it.

Q: What kind of dreams?

A: About the women and children in my sleep. Some days. . . some nights, I can't even sleep. I just lay there thinking about it.

Antiwar Movement

Although U.S. military commanders insisted that they were winning the war, the Viet Cong and North Vietnamese pressed on. Then the Tet offensive in early 1968 shattered the optimism of the American military. Ignoring a truce celebrating the lunar new year, the North Vietnamese launched a carefully orchestrated series of assaults around the country. As the fighting intensified, Americans at home watched images on television more graphic than ever before. One scene, on NBC News, showed General Nguyen Ngoc Loan, chief of the South Vietnamese police, lifting his gun and calmly blowing out the brains of a captive Viet Cong prisoner. A still photograph of the scene won a 1969 Pulitzer Prize.

Meanwhile, a ferocious bombing campaign accompanied the ground fighting. Fragmentation bombs killed and maimed countless civilians. Napalm, a burning jelly that

Breaking Point

My Lai was the worst episode of soldiers losing control, but it was not the only one. Marine Philip Caputo described a frightening incident during his service in Vietnam when his platoon, anxious for revenge and retribution for friends now dead, entered a village and exploded in a murderous rage:

"Then it happened. The platoon exploded. It was a collective emotional detonation of men who had been pushed to the extremity of endurance. I lost control of them and even of myself. Desperate to get to the hill, we rampaged through the rest of the village, whooping like savages, torching thatch huts, tossing grenades into the cement houses we could not burn."

Posters popularized the antiwar movement. One of the best-known posters of the period used a simple drawing and bold, childlike lettering to convey its message.

sears off human flesh, was equally widely used, leaving numerous victims in its wake. Even children faced the horrors of war. In one widely circulated photograph that also won a Pulitzer Prize, a group of terrified children ran down a highway after a bombing raid. Nine-year-old Kim Phuc had just torn off her napalm-burned clothing, along with some of her own seared-off skin, in a futile effort to escape the attack.

Such pictures, and others on the evening news, helped create growing opposition to the war at home. Students were among the first to question the cold war assumptions about the need to combat communism around the world. The first teach-in where students and faculty members debated issues about Vietnam took place at the University of Michigan in March 1965, soon after escalation of the war had begun. Featuring both supporters and opponents of the war, it was an effort to explore different aspects of the problem. But as other teach-ins followed on college campuses around the country, supporters of the war effort became less welcome and the sessions became in effect antiwar rallies.

The antiwar movement came to include a wide variety of people. Boxer Muhammad Ali legitimated draft resistance when he argued that his Islamic religion prohibited his involvement in war and refused to be inducted into military service. Women, though not subject to the draft, became a powerful source of opposition. And students remained at the forefront of the struggle. In 1967, some 300,000 people marched against the war in New York City and 100,000 tried to close down the Pentagon.

The anthem of the antiwar movement became the "I-Feel-Like-I'm-Fixin'-to-Die Rag," written by Joe McDonald in 1964 and recorded by Country Joe and the Fish in 1967:

Come on all of you big strong men,
Uncle Sam needs your help again;
He's got himself in a terrible jam
Way down yonder in Viet Nam;
So put down your books and pick
   up a gun,
We're gonna have a whole lot of fun!
Chorus:

NBC's John Chancellor provided the following commentary when the network aired this image: "There was awful savagery. . . . Here the infamous chief of the South Vietnamese National Police, General Loan, executed a captured Viet Cong officer.— Rough justice on a Saigon street as the charmed life of the city of Saigon comes to a bloody end." The images of the war that Americans watched at dinnertime on the television news or saw in newspapers and magazines appalled them, and played a major role in mobilizing opposition to the war.

Despite hopes for a clean and crisp military victory, the war had a devastating impact on the human population. Kim Phuc (center) survived this bombing raid but required 17 operations to heal her body, which still left her with thick white scars on her neck, arm, and back. Years later, in November 1996, as she spoke at a Veterans Day observance in Washington, D.C., she met the pilot who had ordered the bombing strike. As he apologized profusely for the attack, which still haunted him, she responded, "It's all right. I forgive. I forgive."

And it's one two three
What are we fighting for?
Don't ask me, I don't give a damn,
Next stop is Vietnam.
And it's five six seven,
Open up the Pearly Gates;
There ain't no time to wonder why,
Whoopie—we're all gonna die!

Come on, generals, let's move fast,
Your big chance has come at last;
Now you can go out and get those Reds,
The only good Commie is one that's dead;
You know that peace can only be won,
When we've blown 'em all to kingdom come!
Chorus
Come on, Wall Street, don't be slow,
Why, man, this is war Au-go-go;
There's plenty good money to be made,
Supplying the army with tools of the trade;
Just hope and pray if they drop the Bomb,
They drop it on the Viet Cong!
Chorus

To live is to give oneself to the fatherland,
It is to give oneself to the earth, the mountains
  and to the rivers
It is to clench one's teeth in the face of the
  enemy,
To live is to keep up one's courage in times of
  misery,
It is to laugh in times of anger,
To live is to remain optimistic in the struggle,
It is to crush, it is to break the image of the
  enemy,
One must drink passionately of the blood of
  the enemy.

—A diary entry found with Lieutenant Dao
An Tuat of the North Vietnamese Army after
his death

Come on, mothers, throughout the land,
Pack your boys off to Vietnam;
Come on, fathers, don't hesitate,
Send your sons off before it's too late;
You can be the first one on your block
To have your boy come home in a box.
Chorus

Vietnamization

The intensity of the antiwar protest and the rift it caused in the United States finally persuaded Lyndon Johnson not to run for re-election in 1968. He withdrew from the race and began negotiations with the North Vietnamese. But not even a bombing halt could bring about a settlement. As the Democratic Party self-destructed, the way was cleared for Republican Richard Nixon to win the Presidency.

Nixon claimed to have a secret plan to end the war, but such a scheme never became evident. Instead, he moved to end the draft and bring American soldiers home in a policy called Vietnamization, whereby the Vietnamese themselves would take over responsibility for the conduct of the war. For a time Nixon defused the antiwar protests until he decided, in the spring of 1970, to widen the war by attacking sanctuaries in neighboring countries, particularly Cambodia, from which the North Vietnamese were launching attacks on South Vietnam. The resulting firestorm of protest caused further disruptions on college campuses, but Nixon pressed on with the military campaign.

Ten days ago, in my report to the Nation on Vietnam, I announced a decision to withdraw an additional 150,000 Americans from Vietnam over the next year. I said then that I was making that decision despite our concern over increased enemy activity in Laos, in Cambodia, and in South Vietnam.

At that time, I warned that if I concluded that increased enemy activity in any of these areas endangered the lives of Americans remaining in Vietnam, I would not hesitate to take strong and effective measures to deal with that situation.

Despite that warning, North Vietnam has increased its military aggression in all these areas, and particularly in Cambodia. . . .

To protect our men who are in Vietnam and to guarantee the continued success of our withdrawal and Vietnamization programs, I have concluded that the time has come for action. . . .

Lyndon Johnson thought it inconceivable that the powerful United States could lose the war in Vietnam, but he saw it undermine his Presidency. Here he shows his anguish as he listens to a tape recording made by his son-in-law, Marine Chuck Robb, describing his personal experiences in the war.

Now confronted with this situation, we have three options.

First, we can do nothing. Well, the ultimate result of that course of action is clear. Unless we indulge in wishful thinking, the lives of Americans remaining in Vietnam after our next withdrawal of 150,000 would be gravely threatened. . . .

Our second choice is to provide massive military assistance to Cambodia itself. Now, unfortunately, while we deeply sympathize with the plight of 7 million Cambodians whose country is being invaded, massive amounts of military assistance could not be rapidly and effectively utilized by the small Cambodian Army against the immediate threat. . . .

Our third choice is to go to the heart of the trouble. That means cleaning out major North Vietnamese and Vietcong occupied territories—these sanctuaries which serve as bases for attacks on both Cambodia and American and South Vietnamese forces in South Vietnam. . . .

Now faced with these three options, this is the decision I have made.

In cooperation with the armed forces of South Vietnam, attacks are being launched this week to clean out major enemy sanctuaries on the Cambodian–Vietnam border. . . .

My fellow Americans, we live in an age of anarchy, both abroad and at home. We see mindless attacks on all the great institutions which have been created by free civilizations in the last 500 years. Even here in the United States, great universities are being systematically destroyed. Small nations all over the world find themselves under attack from within and from without.

Richard Nixon's announcement that he was widening the war and moving into Cambodia brought renewed antiwar activity at colleges and universities. At Kent State University in Ohio, after students burned the building where the army trained reserve officers, the National Guard mobilized on the campus and later fired on the students without provocation, killing four and wounding nine.

Kissinger brought peace to Vietnam the same way that Napoleon brought peace to Europe in the early 19th century: by losing.

—Post–Vietnam War joke

Americans assumed throughout the cold war, and during the war in Vietnam, that their democratic system could work anywhere in the world. The bitter experience in Southeast Asia demonstrated that people in other countries had their own priorities and might not want to follow in the footsteps of the United States.

If, when the chips are down, the world's most powerful nation, the United States of America, acts like a pitiful, helpless giant, the forces of totalitarianism and anarchy will threaten free nations and free institutions throughout the world. . . .

Reunification

Vietnam remained a political football as Nixon ran for re-election in 1972. Negotiations seemed to promise a settlement to the war—just days before the election, Secretary of State Henry Kissinger promised that peace was at hand. But when South Vietnam balked at the settlement, the United States launched the most intensive bombing campaign of the war. Hanoi was hit, and mines were planted in North Vietnamese harbors. Only in the new year was a cease-fire and agreement to end the war, excerpted here, finally signed. For the United States the war was over, even if the settlement left Vietnam divided. Three years later, the North Vietnamese reunified the country on their own terms and the war was in fact over at last.

The Parties participating in the Paris Conference on Vietnam,

With a view to ending the war and restoring peace in Vietnam on the basis of respect for the Vietnamese people's fundamental national rights and the South Vietnamese people's right to self-determination, and to contributing to the consolidation of peace in Asia and the world,

Have agreed on the following provisions and undertake to respect and to implement them:

Chapter I
The Vietnamese People's Fundamental Rights
Article 1
The United States and all other countries respect the independence, sovereignty, unity, and territorial integrity of Vietnam as recognized by the 1954 Geneva Agreements on Vietnam.

Chapter II
Cessation of Hostilities—Withdrawal of Troops
Article 2
A cease-fire shall be observed throughout South Vietnam as of 2400 hours G.M.T., [Greenwich, England, Mean Time] on January 27, 1973.

At the same hour, the United States will stop all its military activities against the territory of the Democratic Republic of Vietnam by ground, air and naval forces, wherever they may be based, and end the mining of the territorial waters, ports, harbors, and waterways of the Democratic Republic of Vietnam. The United States will remove, permanently deactivate or destroy all the mines in the territorial waters, ports, harbors, and waterways of North Vietnam as soon as this Agreement goes into effect. . . .

The Vietnam War had savage consequences. It was the longest war in U.S. history and led to more than 58,000 American deaths. It cost more than $150 billion but was still unsuccessful. And it tore the nation apart. Reconciliation came slowly, but the building of the Vietnam Veterans Memorial in Washington, D.C., dedicated in 1982, helped the healing process. The stark simplicity of the black granite walls, tapering to a V, with the names of the dead inscribed chronologically by date of death, provided a sense of peace for people visiting from around the world. The Washington Monument is visible in the distance.

Article 6

The dismantlement of all military bases in South Vietnam of the United States and of . . . other foreign countries . . . shall be completed within sixty days of the signing of this Agreement. . . .

Chapter IV
The Exercise of the South Vietnamese People's Right to Self-Determination
Article 9

The Government of the United States of America and the Government of the Democratic Republic of Vietnam undertake to respect the following principles for the exercise of the South Vietnamese people's right to self-determination:

(a) The South Vietnamese people's right to self-determination is sacred, inalienable, and shall be respected by all countries.

(b) The South Vietnamese people shall decide themselves the political future of South Vietnam through genuinely free and democratic general elections under international supervision.

(c) Foreign countries shall not impose any political tendency or personality on the South Vietnamese people. . . .

Chapter V
The Reunification of Vietnam and the Relationship between North and South Vietnam
Article 15

The reunification of Vietnam shall be carried out step by step through peaceful means on the basis of discussions and agreements between North and South Vietnam, without coercion or annexation by either party, and without foreign interference. The time for reunification will be agreed upon by North and South Vietnam. . . .

Chapter Six

An End at Last

At long last, after almost 50 years, the cold war came to an end. Efforts at reconciliation had eased tension at a number of points in the past, and agreements between the Soviet Union and the United States had limited nuclear testing and mandated the first steps toward arms control. But relations had deteriorated each time, leaving the world as unsafe and unstable as before.

Then, in the 1980s, the bitter conflict suddenly ceased. A massive American increase in military spending, which forced the Soviets to spend more than they could afford in an effort to keep up, coupled with a Russian effort to ease internal restrictions, brought Soviet society to a breaking point. As the U.S.S.R. could no longer maintain the tight discipline it had imposed for decades in Eastern Europe, satellite nations began to splinter off. The disintegration, which spread to the Soviet Union itself, brought about a similar fragmentation there, resulting in independence for its member republics like Ukraine and Belarus. By the early 1990s, the United States suddenly found itself standing alone, the only superpower in the world.

This dramatic turn of events caught American policy makers by surprise. They had made all their decisions in the post–World War II years with an eye toward maintaining balance in the fragile and dangerous cold war arena. Now they had to craft new ways of dealing with nations around the globe—including the remnants of the Soviet Union—to establish a new and different kind of world order.

The Limited Test Ban Treaty of 1963

The first real effort to work together came with the Limited Test-Ban Treaty of 1963. Pressures to end nuclear testing to eliminate radioactive fallout had culminated in a voluntary moratorium in 1958 that lasted until the early 1960s. But when diplomatic relations deteriorated again, the United States and the Soviet Union found themselves testing and stockpiling new weapons in ever-increasing numbers. Both nations subscribed to the policy of deterrence, in which one power's nuclear forces were intended

Russian President Boris Yeltsin, standing between President George Bush and his wife Barbara in front of the White House, enjoyed a close personal relationship with the American leader in the aftermath of the cold war. Yeltsin presided over the transition to capitalism in Russia, the largest of the republics that became autonomous as the Soviet Union split apart in the early 1990s.

to prevent the other from using its atomic weapons in what would be an unwinnable war for both. Such a conflict, if it occurred, would lead to "mutual assured destruction," with the acronym MAD reflecting the folly of that approach. The Cuban missile crisis in 1962, which brought the world closer than ever before to nuclear war, demonstrated that it might not be possible to maintain an atomic equilibrium and highlighted the urgency of finding a solution to the nuclear dilemma.

As the Cuban missile crisis wound down, both President John F. Kennedy and Soviet leader Nikita Khrushchev acknowledged the need to find a way to control nuclear weapons. The main stumbling block to a test-ban treaty was verification, or setting up a means to ensure that the other side was following the rules. The United States insisted on the right to conduct inspections on Russian soil to ensure compliance with any agreement, but the Soviets argued that such monitoring was actually spying. In late 1962, Khrushchev agreed to allow two or three on-site inspections,

As the Cuban missile crisis came to an end, both American and Soviet leaders recognized the need for closer communication to avoid a similar episode in the future. The United States proposed, and the Soviet Union accepted, a "hot line" teletype link that would remain open and available at all times.

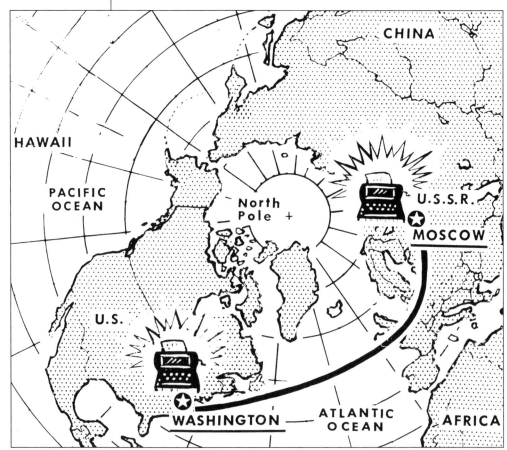

although Kennedy held out for 8 or even 10. The next spring, in a speech at American University's commencement in Washington, D.C., Kennedy broke the diplomatic deadlock by underscoring the need for people to live together and announcing that the United States would not conduct further nuclear tests in the atmosphere as long as other nations refrained as well. He also appointed a negotiator to work with the Soviet Union and Britain. After a few weeks of discussions, the Limited Test Ban Treaty, signed in Moscow on August 5, 1963, and ratified by the Senate two months later, was the result.

The Governments of the United States of America, the United Kingdom of Great Britain and Northern Ireland, and the Union of Soviet Socialist Republics, hereinafter referred to as the "Original Parties",

Proclaiming as their principal aim the speediest possible achievement of an agreement on general and complete disarmament under strict international control in accordance with the objectives of the United Nations which would put an end to the armaments race and eliminate the incentive to the production and testing of all kinds of weapons, including nuclear weapons,

Seeking to achieve the discontinuance of all test explosions of nuclear weapons for all time, determined to continue negotiations to this end, and desiring to put an end to the contamination of man's environment by radioactive substances,

Have agreed as follows:

Article I

1. Each of the Parties to this Treaty undertakes to prohibit, to prevent, and not to carry out any nuclear weapon test explosion, or any other nuclear explosion, at any place under its jurisdiction or control:

(a) in the atmosphere; beyond its limits, including outer space; or under water, including territorial waters or high seas; or

(b) in any other environment if such explosion causes radioactive debris to be present outside the territorial limits of the State under whose jurisdiction or control such explosion is conducted. It is understood in this connection that the provisions of this subparagraph are without prejudice to the conclusion of a treaty resulting in the permanent banning of all nuclear test explosions, including all such explosions underground, the conclusion of which, as the Parties have stated in the Preamble of this Treaty, they seek to achieve.

The Limited Test Ban Treaty of 1963 was the first formal agreement to end certain kinds of nuclear testing. This cartoon shows British Prime Minister Harold Macmillan, President Kennedy, and Soviet leader Khrushchev (left to right, at bottom), all signers of the pact, with Chairman Mao Zedong of China and President Charles de Gaulle of France (left and right, at top) objecting to the treaty.

Look, this is an awfully dangerous world. I didn't think you would do this and you obviously didn't think I would react as I did. This is too dangerous a way for us to go on.

— President Kennedy to Anastas Mikoyan, a top Soviet official, at the end of the Cuban missile crisis, in a conversation recalled by Presidential advisor Walt W. Rostow

2. Each of the parties to this Treaty undertakes furthermore to refrain from causing, encouraging, or in any way participating in, the carrying out of any nuclear weapon test explosion, or any other nuclear explosion, anywhere which would take place in any of the environments described, or have the effect referred to, in paragraph 1 of this Article. . . .

SALT Treaties

Richard Nixon took the next step toward weapons control when he assumed the Presidency in 1969. Facing deep divisions in a country torn apart by the Vietnam War, Nixon wanted to restore national and international stability. Although he was suspicious at first of seeming to appear weak by being willing to compromise, he soon came to realize that a nuclear pact could rest at the center of a network of contacts with the Soviet Union. Arms control could provide the "linkage" for all the elements of his foreign policy.

Thirty months after negotiations called the Strategic Arms Limitation Talks (SALT) began, the SALT I Treaty was the result. Signed in Moscow on May 26, 1972, and ratified by the Senate several months later, the SALT I Treaty included an agreement restricting each nation to developing and deploying two antiballistic missile systems, on the ground that such defensive systems might encourage a nation to launch a pre-emptive strike. There was also an interim agreement

After signing the SALT I agreements in 1972, President Richard Nixon (center, left), standing with Soviet General Secretary Leonid Brezhnev (right), continued discussions at a Washington summit in 1973. There the leaders explored initiatives for economic and cultural exchange and began to consider further arms reduction measures.

**for five years that set ceilings on intercontinental and other
ballistic missiles in an effort to find a point where the two
nations would be relatively evenly matched.**

Treaty Between the United States of America and the Union of
Soviet Socialist Republics on the Limitation of Anti-Ballistic Missile Systems

The United States of America and the Union of Soviet Socialist Republics, hereinafter referred to as the Parties,

Proceeding from the premise that nuclear war would have devastating consequences for all mankind,

Considering that effective measures to limit anti-ballistic missile systems would be a substantial factor in curbing the race in strategic offensive arms and would lead to a decrease in the risk of outbreak of war involving nuclear weapons,

Proceeding from the premise that the limitation of anti-ballistic missile systems, as well as certain agreed measures with respect to the limitation of strategic offensive arms, would contribute to the creation of more favorable conditions for further negotiations on limiting strategic arms, . . .

Declaring their intention to achieve at the earliest possible date the cessation of the nuclear arms race and to take effective measures toward reductions in strategic arms, nuclear disarmament, and general and complete disarmament,

Desiring to contribute to the relaxation of international tension and the strengthening of trust between States,

Have agreed as follows:

Article I

1. Each Party undertakes to limit anti-ballistic missile (ABM) systems and to adopt other measures in accordance with the provision of this Treaty.

2. Each party undertakes not to deploy ABM systems for a defense of the territory of its country and not to provide a base for such a defense, and not to deploy ABM systems for defense of an individual region except as provided for in Article III [permitting two systems] of this Treaty.

Article II

1. For the Purpose of this Treaty an ABM system is a system to counter strategic ballistic missiles or their elements in flight trajectory. . . .

Multiple-exposure photography shows the U.S. army's Pershing ballistic missile rising into firing position. The missile, designed to carry conventional or nuclear warheads, was photographed at the army's missile test center in Huntsville, Alabama, in 1963.

As he negotiated with Soviet leader Leonid Brezhnev, Nixon watched his counterpart carefully and observed: "Despite the impatience he affected with the details and numbers, Brezhnev was obviously very well briefed on the subject. He used a red pencil to sketch missiles on the notepad in front of him as we discussed the timing and techniques of control and limitation."

As he negotiated with the Soviet Union, Richard Nixon made overtures to the People's Republic of China as well. In 1972, he traveled to China, where he met with Chinese leaders, ate meals and drank toasts with Chinese officials, and paved the way for the formal diplomatic recognition by the United States in subsequent years.

Interim Agreement Between the United States of America and the Union of Soviet Socialist Republics on Certain Measures with Respect to the Limitation of Strategic Offensive Arms

The United States of America and the Union of Soviet Socialist Republics, hereinafter referred to as the Parties,

Convinced that the Treaty on the Limitation of Anti-Ballistic Missile Systems and this Interim Agreement on Certain Measures with Respect to the Limitation of Strategic Offensive Arms will contribute to the creation of more favorable conditions for active negotiations on limiting strategic arms as well as to the relaxation of international tension and the strengthening of trust between States,

Taking into account the relationship between strategic offensive and defensive arms, . . .

Have agreed as follows:

Article I

The Parties undertake not to start construction of additional fixed land-based intercontinental ballistic missile (ICBM) launchers after July 1, 1972.

Article II

The Parties undertake not to convert land-based launchers for light ICBMs, or for ICBMs of older types deployed prior to 1964, into land-based launchers for heavy ICBMs of types deployed after that time.

Article III

The Parties undertake to limit submarine-launched ballistic missile (SLBM) launchers and modern ballistic missile submarines to the numbers operational and under construction on the date of signature of this Interim Agreement, and in addition to launchers and submarines constructed under procedures established by the Parties as replacements for an equal number of ICBM launchers of older types deployed prior to 1964 or for launchers on older submarines. . . .

Because the interim agreement was to last only five years, negotiations for a new pact began almost immediately. President Jimmy Carter, who took office in 1977, supported a SALT II Treaty, and negotiations culminated in a document signed in Vienna, Austria, on June 18, 1979. This treaty began with the preamble reproduced here, which was then followed by detailed restrictions far more complex than those in previous treaties.

While SALT II was a step forward, it met with a chilly response in the United States. Supporters of arms control claimed that it legitimized arms competition. Opponents contended that it gave too much away. With the Senate divided, the Soviet invasion of Afghanistan, on its southern border, killed any possibility of ratification, for legislators were afraid of seeming to approve of the incursion, and Carter withdrew the treaty. The episode indicated that the cold war was still very much alive.

The United States of America and the Union of Soviet Socialist Republics, hereinafter referred to as the Parties,

Conscious that nuclear war would have devastating consequences for all mankind, . . .

Attaching particular significance to the limitation of strategic arms and determined to continue their efforts begun with the Treaty on the Limitation of Anti-Ballistic Missile Systems and the Interim Agreement on Certain Measures with Respect to the Limitation of Strategic Offensive Arms, of May 26, 1972,

Convinced that the additional measures limiting strategic offensive arms provided for in this Treaty will contribute to the improvement of relations between the Parties, help to reduce the risk of outbreak of nuclear war and strengthen international peace and security, . . .

Nuclear war cannot be measured by the archaic standards of victory and defeat. This stark reality imposes on the United States and the Soviet Union an awesome and special responsibility.

—President Jimmy Carter, calling for further nuclear arms limitation in an address to the United Nations General Assembly in his first year of office

In 1979 President Jimmy Carter and Soviet leader Leonid Brezhnev signed the SALT II accord, which extended the arms control process. But the Soviet invasion of Afghanistan led the U.S. Senate to refuse to ratify the treaty, and so it was never formally implemented.

Guided by the principle of equality and equal security,

Recognizing that the strengthening of strategic stability meets the interests of the Parties and the interests of international security,

Reaffirming their desire to take measures for the further limitation and for the further reduction of strategic arms, having in mind the goal of achieving general and complete disarmament,

Declaring their intention to undertake in the near future negotiations further to limit and further to reduce strategic offensive arms,

Have agreed as follows: . . .

Here followed page after page specifying caps on the number of warheads that could be placed on missiles, limiting the numbers of multiple-warheaded missiles, and freezing the number of weapons-delivery systems permitted.

Fears of a nuclear holocaust mounted again in the 1980s as American relations with the Soviet Union deteriorated. In 1983, the television film The Day After, *set in metropolitan Kansas City, showed missiles exploding from silos, bombs detonating, and bodies vaporizing on screen.*

Reagan's Nuclear Strategy

Diplomatic relations between the United States and the Soviet Union deteriorated in the 1980s. Shortly before leaving office, Jimmy Carter signed Presidential Directive-59, which committed the United States to fight a prolonged nuclear war that might last for months, rather than days or weeks. In his first year as President, Ronald Reagan took that commitment one step further with National Security Division Directive-13, which committed the nation to winning a nuclear war. Scenarios of nuclear catastrophe became commonplace.

U.S. policy further contributed to the revived cold war tensions. To support its militant approach toward the Soviet Union, the Reagan administration sought an unprecedented $1.5 trillion over a five-year period to support a massive arms buildup. The President contended that the nation was militarily vulnerable and must therefore spend whatever was necessary to bolster its arsenal of both nuclear and conventional weapons.

In response, critics demanded a nuclear freeze to limit the ever-increasing supply of nuclear arms. Two dozen Senators and more than 150 Congressmen sponsored a resolution endorsing such a mutual and verifiable arms freeze. They were troubled by the failure of SALT II, even if the United States had observed some of the limitations on its own, and worried

President Reagan's security directive was a top-secret document, but a document providing the essentials was leaked to the press. It stated that "should deterrence fail and strategic nuclear war with the U.S.S.R. occur, the United States must prevail and be able to force the Soviet Union to seek earliest termination of hostilities favorable to the United States."

when Reagan discarded past diplomatic efforts in favor of what he called START—Strategic Arms Reduction Talks.

Reagan made his opposition to a freeze clear in a speech to a group of church leaders of the National Association of Evangelicals, meeting at a convention in Orlando, Florida, in 1983. In that speech, he called the Soviet Union an "evil empire," making a casual reference to the popular *Star Wars* film.

The truth is that a freeze now would be a very dangerous fraud, for that is merely the illusion of peace. The reality is that we must find peace through strength.

I would agree to a freeze if only we could freeze the Soviets' global desires. A freeze at current levels of weapons would remove any incentive for the Soviets to negotiate seriously at Geneva and virtually end our chances to achieve the major arms reductions which we have proposed. Instead, they would achieve their objectives through the freeze.

A freeze would reward the Soviet Union for its enormous and unparalleled military buildup. It would prevent the essential and long overdue modernization of United States and allied defenses and would leave our aging forces increasingly vulnerable. And an honest freeze would require extensive prior negotiations on the systems and numbers to be limited and on the measures to ensure effective verification and compliance. And the kind of a freeze that has been suggested would be virtually impossible to verify. Such a major effort would divert us completely from our current negotiations on achieving substantial reductions. . . .

So, I urge you to speak out against those who would place the United States in a position of military and moral inferiority. . . . In your discussions of the nuclear freeze proposals, I urge you to beware the temptation of pride—the temptation of blithely declaring yourselves above it all and label[ing] both sides equally at fault, to

In the midst of a massive military buildup and increasingly antagonistic international relations, children in the Reagan era were confronted with the possibility of atomic annihilation. Some wrote letters to the President expressing their anxiety.

President Reagan,
Why do you want to kill harmless children?
Why do you make new bombs? Why do you want to destory the only world, why?

Singed Brian

Backlash

New York Times columnist Russell Baker, responding to the aggressive efforts of the Reagan administration to discredit the nuclear freeze proposal, wrote, "My position on the nuclear freeze is that the government ought to stop telling me I'm too dumb to have an opinion on it."

ignore the facts of history and aggressive impulses of an evil empire, to simply call the arms race a giant misunderstanding and thereby remove yourself from the struggle between right and wrong and good and evil. . . .

Although he was opposed to a freeze, President Reagan recognized the need to counter Americans' anxiety about a potential nuclear attack. He had long fantasized about special defensive weapons that could protect the nation. Many years earlier in the film *Murder in the Air*, he had played Secret Service agent Brass Bancroft, whose mission was to defend a new superweapon—a "death-ray projector"—that could stop enemy planes. Now, just two weeks after calling the Soviet Union an "evil empire," he proposed a new kind of nuclear shield in space—a kind of space-based nuclear umbrella—that could destroy Russian missiles before they reached the United States. The plan, called the Strategic Defense Initiative, was quickly dubbed Star Wars, again after the popular film. At the end of a speech to the nation about defense and national security, Reagan outlined his expansive vision.

Critics argued that President Ronald Reagan's Star Wars proposal for satellites in outer space that could shoot down incoming missiles would never work. Reagan persisted in supporting the initiative and Congress provided some money to explore the possibility of developing such a system in the 1980s and 1990s. This Department of Defense picture was used to illustrate the potential of the Strategic Defense Initiative.

Let me share with you a vision of the future which offers hope. It is that we embark on a program to counter the awesome Soviet missile threat with measures that are defensive. Let us turn to the very strengths in technology that spawned our great industrial base and that have given us the quality of life we enjoy today.

What if free people could live secure in the knowledge that their security did not rest upon the threat of instant U.S. retaliation to deter a Soviet attack, that we could intercept and destroy strategic ballistic missiles before they reached our own soil or that of our allies?

I know this is a formidable, technical task, one that may not be accomplished before the end of this century. Yet, current technology has attained a level of sophistication where it's reasonable for us to begin this effort. It will take years, probably decades of effort on many fronts. There will be failures and setbacks, just as there will be successes and breakthroughs. And as we proceed, we must remain constant in preserving the nuclear deterrent

President Reagan and Soviet General Secretary Mikhail Gorbachev worked well together. As Gorbachev, seated on the right at a summit meeting in Geneva, Switzerland, recognized that the Soviet Union needed to cut back its military spending, his overtures to the United States led to a number of important arms control agreements.

and maintaining a solid capability for flexible response. But isn't it worth every investment necessary to free the world from the threat of nuclear war? We know it is. . . .

Tonight. . . I'm taking an important first step. I am directing a comprehensive and intensive effort to define a long-term research and development program to begin to achieve our ultimate goal of eliminating the threat posed by strategic nuclear missiles. This could pave the way for arms control measures to eliminate the weapons themselves. We seek neither military superiority nor political advantage. Our only purpose—one all people share—is to search for ways to reduce the danger of nuclear war.

An End to the Cold War

Mikhail Gorbachev, the new Soviet leader who assumed power in 1985, recognized the need for accommodation with the West. He endorsed policies of *glasnost* (political openness to encourage personal initiative) and *perestroika* (restructuring the economy), and signed the Intermediate-Range Nuclear Forces Treaty with Ronald Reagan in 1987 and the Strategic Arms Reduction Treaty (START) with George Bush in 1991. But his liberalization policies caused problems for Gorbachev at home and led to successful independence

Critics argued that President Reagan's Star Wars effort would be incredibly expensive and was doomed to fail. Some proposed their own acronyms for the new program: DUMB (Defensive Umbrella) and WACKO (Wistful Attempts to Circumvent Killing Ourselves).

The destruction of the Berlin Wall served as a symbolic blow to the entire cold war. As people crushed the concrete and piled over the rubble, joyous celebrations erupted spontaneously on both sides of what had been an almost insurmountable barricade. Germans from both sides of the Berlin Wall destroyed the 12-foot-high barrier, singing their own version of the song "For He's a Jolly Good Fellow."

movements in the Baltic republics of Latvia, Lithuania, and Estonia. Then the process of disintegration spread throughout Eastern Europe. The head of the East German Communist Party announced in November 1989 that people there would be free to leave the country. Within hours, thousands of Germans gathered on both sides of the hated 28-mile-long Berlin Wall and celebrated. Within days, they had taken sledgehammers and smashed it down.

In 1990, President George Bush announced his dream of "a new world order," a phrase that was picked up and repeated in the months and years that followed. Now all that remained was to declare an end to the cold war. In early 1992, in his State of the Union Address, Bush announced what everyone already knew: that the cold war was over and the United States had won.

The collapse of communism in Eastern Europe occurred quickly. In Washington, D.C., the CIA director, William H. Webster, admitted with surprise, "It is going much faster than anyone might have anticipated."

We gather tonight at a dramatic and deeply promising time in our history and in the history of man on Earth. For in the past 12 months, the world has known changes of almost Biblical proportions. And even now, months after the failed coup that doomed a failed system, I'm not sure we've absorbed the full impact, the full import of what happened. But communism died this year.

Even as President, with the most fascinating possible vantage point, there were times when I was so busy managing progress and helping to lead change that I didn't always show the joy that was in my heart. But the biggest thing that has happened in the world in my life, in our lives, is this: By the grace of God, America won the cold war.

I mean to speak this evening of the changes that can take place in our country, now that we can stop making the sacrifices we had to make when we had an avowed enemy that was a superpower. Now we can look homeward even more and move to set right what needs to be set right.

I will speak of those things. But let me tell you something I've been thinking these past few months. It's a kind of rollcall of honor. For the cold war didn't end; it was won. And I think of those who won it, in places like Korea and Vietnam. And some of them didn't come back. Back then they were heroes, but this year they were victors. . . .

Several days after Bush's State of the Union Address, he met with Russian leader Boris Yeltsin. In a joint press conference, Bush declared: "This historic meeting is yet another confirmation of the end of the cold war and the dawn of a new era." Yeltsin concurred, saying: "From now on, we do not consider ourselves to be potential enemies as it had been previously in our military doctrine."

President George Bush (front left), continued to work closely with Soviet leader Mikhail Gorbachev, just as Ronald Reagan had done. The START agreement they signed in Moscow in 1991 further advanced the effort to control nuclear arms.

Timeline

1945
United States drops first atomic bombs on Hiroshima and Nagasaki in Japan; Franklin D. Roosevelt dies and Harry S. Truman becomes President

1946
Joseph Stalin declares that communism will triumph over capitalism; Winston Churchill delivers his "iron curtain" speech

1947
Truman Doctrine provides aid to Greece and Turkey; House Un-American Activities Committee (HUAC) investigates the movie industry

1948
Marshall Plan provides massive economic aid to Europe; Berlin Airlift provides supplies to western sector of the city; Hiss–Chambers case begins

1949
Soviet Union tests an atomic bomb; North Atlantic Treaty Organization (NATO) established; communist forces triumph in Chinese civil war

1950
Joseph McCarthy makes speech about subversion in Wheeling, West Virginia; NSC-68 approved; Korean War begins

1952
Dwight D. Eisenhower is elected President

1953
Joseph Stalin dies and Nikita Khrushchev consolidates power in Soviet Union; Julius and Ethel Rosenberg are executed as spies

1954
Fall of Dien Bien Phu ends French role in Vietnam; Geneva Conference partitions Vietnam; Army–McCarthy hearings take place; Bravo test of hydrogen bomb highlights danger of fallout

1956
Suez Canal crisis erupts

1957
Russians launch *Sputnik* satellite

1960
John F. Kennedy is elected President

1961
Bay of Pigs invasion in Cuba fails; Berlin Wall is built

1962
Cuban missile crisis unfolds

1963
Buddhists begin demonstrations in Vietnam; John F. Kennedy is assassinated and Lyndon B. Johnson becomes President; United States, Great Britain, and Soviet Union sign Limited Test Ban Treaty

WESTMINSTER COLLEGE
Harry Truman
Winston Churchill
FULTON, MO. 1946

1964

Congress passes Gulf of Tonkin resolution

1968

Tet offensive occurs in Vietnam; Richard Nixon is elected President

1970

United States widens war in Vietnam with invasion of Cambodia; National Guard kills students at Kent State University

1972

Nixon visits People's Republic of China; United States and Soviet Union sign SALT I treaty on nuclear arms

1973

Vietnam cease-fire is signed

1975

South Vietnam is defeated by North Vietnam and war in Vietnam ends

1976

Jimmy Carter is elected President

1979

Nuclear accident occurs at Three Mile Island power plant; United States and Soviet Union sign SALT II treaty on nuclear arms

1980

Ronald Reagan is elected President

1983

Reagan proposes Strategic Defense Initiative (Star Wars plan)

1987

United States and Soviet Union sign Intermediate-Range Nuclear Forces Treaty

1988

George Bush is elected President

1989

Berlin Wall is smashed

1991

United States and Soviet Union sign Strategic Arms Reduction Treaty (START); Soviet Union splits apart into its component republics

1992

Bush announces the end of the cold war and American victory

Further Reading

Overviews

Ambrose, Stephen E. *Rise to Globalism: American Foreign Policy Since 1938*, 3rd rev. ed. New York: Penguin, 1983.

Gaddis, John Lewis. *We Now Know: Rethinking Cold War History*. New York: Oxford University Press, 1997.

LaFeber, Walter. *America, Russia, and the Cold War, 1945–1996*, 8th ed. New York: McGraw-Hill, 1997.

Levering, Ralph B. *The Cold War: A Post–Cold War History*. Arlington Heights, Ill.: Harlan Davidson, 1994.

McCormick, Thomas J. *America's Half Century: United States Foreign Policy in the Cold War*. Baltimore: Johns Hopkins University Press, 1992.

Powaski, Ronald E. *The Cold War: The United States and the Soviet Union, 1917–1991*. New York: Oxford University Press, 1998.

Origins of the Cold War

Gaddis, John Lewis. *The United States and the Origins of the Cold War, 1941–1947*. New York: Columbia University Press, 1972.

Hogan, Michael J. *A Cross of Iron: Harry S. Truman and the Origins of the National Security State, 1945–1954*. New York: Cambridge University Press, 1998.

Yergin, Daniel. *Shattered Peace: The Origins of the Cold War and the National Security State*. Boston: Houghton Mifflin, 1977.

The Truman Years

Ferrell, Robert H. *Harry S. Truman and the Modern American Presidency*. Boston: Little, Brown, 1983.

Hamby, Alonzo L. *Man of the People: A Life of Harry S. Truman*. New York: Oxford University Press, 1995.

Leffler, Melvyn P. *A Preponderance of Power: National Security, the Truman Administration, and the Cold War*. Stanford, Calif.: Stanford University Press, 1992.

McCullough, David. *Truman*. New York: Simon & Schuster, 1992.

The Korean War

Goulden, Joseph C. *Korea: The Untold Story of the War*. New York: Times Books, 1982.

Kaufman, Burton I. *The Korean War: Challenges in Crisis, Credibility, and Command*. New York: Knopf, 1986.

Rees, David. *Korea: The Limited War*. Baltimore: Penguin, 1970.

The Anticommunist Crusade

Caute, David. *The Great Fear: The Anti-Communist Purge Under Truman and Eisenhower*. New York: Simon and Schuster, 1979.

Haynes, John Earl, and Harvey Klehr. *Venona: Decoding Soviet Espionage in America*. New Haven, Connecticut: Yale University Press, 2000.

Kutler, Stanley I. *The American Inquisition: Justice and Injustice in the Cold War*. New York: Hill & Wang, 1982.

Radosh, Ronald, and Milton, Joyce. *The Rosenberg File: A Search for the Truth*. New York: Holt, Rinehart & Winston, 1984.

Schrecker, Ellen W. *Many Are the Crimes: McCarthyism in America*. New York: Little, Brown, 1998.

Weinstein, Allen. *Perjury: The Hiss-Chambers Case*, rev. ed. New York: Random House, 1997.

Weinstein, Allen, and Alexander Vassiliev. *The Haunted Wood: Soviet Espionage in America—The Stalin Era*. New York: Random House, 1999.

Senator Joseph McCarthy

Griffith, Robert. *The Politics of Fear: Joseph R. McCarthy and the Senate*. Lexington: University Press of Kentucky, 1970.

Oshinsky, David M. *A Conspiracy So Immense: The World of Joe McCarthy*. New York: Free Press, 1983.

Reeves, Thomas C. *The Life and Times of Joe McCarthy: A Biography*. New York: Stein & Day, 1982.

Rovere, Richard H. *Senator Joe McCarthy*. New York: World Publishing, 1960.

The Eisenhower Years

Ambrose, Stephen E. *Eisenhower: The President*. New York: Simon and Schuster, 1984.

Brands, H. W., Jr. *Cold Warriors: Eisenhower's Generation and American Foreign Policy*. New York: Columbia University Press, 1988.

Divine, Robert A. *Eisenhower and the Cold War*. New York: Oxford University Press, 1981.

————. *The Sputnik Challenge: Eisenhower's Response to the Soviet Satellite*. New York: Oxford University Press, 1993.

Greenstein, Fred I. *The Hidden-Hand Presidency: Eisenhower as Leader*. New York: Basic, 1982.

Hoopes, Townsend. *The Devil and John Foster Dulles.* Boston: Little, Brown, 1973.

The Kennedy Years

Chang, Laurence, and Kornbluh, Peter, eds., *The Cuban Missile Crisis, 1962: A National Security Archive Documents Reader.* New York: New Press, 1998.

Fursenko, Aleksandr, and Naftali, Timothy. *One Hell of a Gamble: Khrushchev, Castro, and Kennedy.* New York: Norton, 1997.

May, Ernest R., and Zelikow, Philip D., eds., *The Kennedy Tapes: Inside the White House during the Cuban Missile Crisis.* Cambridge, Mass.: Harvard University Press, 1997.

Parmet, Herbert S. *JFK: The Presidency of John F. Kennedy.* New York: Dial, 1983.

Reeves, Richard. *President Kennedy: Profile of Power.* New York: Simon & Schuster, 1993.

The Cold War and Popular Culture

Henriksen, Margot E. *Dr. Strangelove's America: Society and Culture in the Atomic Age.* Berkeley: University of California Press, 1997.

Rose, Lisle A. *The Cold War Comes to Main Street: America in 1950.* Lawrence: University Press of Kansas, 1999.

Whitfield, Stephen J. *The Culture of the Cold War,* 2nd ed. Baltimore: Johns Hopkins University Press, 1990.

The Atomic Age

Boyer, Paul. *By the Bomb's Early Light: American Thought and Culture at the Dawn of the Atomic Age.* New York: Pantheon, 1985.

Bundy, McGeorge. *Danger and Survival: Choices About the Bomb in the First Fifty Years.* New York: Random House, 1988.

Newhouse, John. *War and Peace in the Nuclear Age.* New York: Knopf, 1989.

Weart, Spencer R. *Nuclear Fear: A History of Images.* Cambridge, Mass.: Harvard University Press, 1988.

Winkler, Allan M. *Life Under a Cloud: American Anxiety About the Atom.* New York: Oxford University Press, 1993.

The War in Vietnam

Appy, Christian G. *Working-Class War: American Combat Soldiers and Vietnam.* Chapel Hill: University of North Carolina Press, 1993.

Gardner, Lloyd C. *Pay Any Price: Lyndon Johnson and the Wars for Vietnam.* Chicago: Ivan R. Dee, 1995.

Herring, George C. *America's Longest War: The United States and Vietnam, 1950–1975,* 3rd ed. New York: McGraw-Hill, 1996.

Hunt, Michael H. *Lyndon Johnson's War: America's Cold War Crusade in Vietnam, 1945–1968.* New York: Hill & Wang, 1996.

Karnow, Stanley. *Vietnam: A History: The First Complete Account of Vietnam at War.* New York: Penguin, 1984.

Sheehan, Neil. *A Bright Shining Lie: John Paul Vann and America in Vietnam.* New York: Random House, 1988.

Arms Control and the End of the Cold War

Gaddis, John Lewis. *The United States and the End of the Cold War: Implications, Reconsiderations, Provocations.* New York: Oxford University Press, 1992.

Harvard Nuclear Study Group (Albert Carnesale, Paul Doty, Stanley Hoffmann, Samuel P. Huntington, Joseph S. Nye, Jr., and Scott D. Sagan). *Living with Nuclear Weapons.* Cambridge, Mass.: Harvard University Press, 1983.

Stanford Arms Control Group. *International Arms Control: Issues and Agreements.* Edited by Coit D. Blacker and Gloria Duffy. Stanford, Calif.: Stanford University Press, 1984.

Text Credits

Main Text

pp. 18–19: Letter from Albert Einstein to F. D. Roosevelt, August 2, 1939. Franklin D. Roosevelt Papers, Franklin D. Roosevelt Library, Hyde Park, N.Y.

pp. 20–21: Associated Press, "Text of Premier Stalin's Election Speech Broadcast by Moscow Radio," *New York Times*, February 10, 1946.

pp. 21–22: *Congressional Record.* 79th Congress, 2nd session, A 1145–1147. Reprinted in Walter LaFeber, ed., *The Origins of the Cold War, 1941–1947.* New York: Wiley, 1971, pp. 135–39.

pp. 23–24: *Foreign Relations of the United States, 1946. Volume VI, Eastern Europe: The Soviet Union.* Washington, D.C.: U.S. Government Printing Office, 1969, pp. 696–709.

pp. 24–26: "X," "The Sources of Soviet Conduct," *Foreign Affairs*, Volume XXV, July 1947, pp. 566–82. Reprinted by permission of FOREIGN AFFAIRS, July 1947. Copyright 1947 by the Council on Foreign Relations, Inc.

pp. 26–29: "Special Message to the Congress on Greece and Turkey: The Truman Doctrine, March 12, 1947," *Public Papers of the Presidents of the United States: Harry S. Truman: 1947.* Washington, D.C.: U.S. Government Printing Office, 1963, pp.176–80.

pp. 29–31: *Department of State Bulletin*, Vol. XVI, June 15, 1947, pp. 1159–1160.

pp. 32–34: "Statement by the President on Announcing the First Atomic Explosion in the U.S.S.R., September 23, 1949," *Public Papers of the Presidents of the United States: Harry S. Truman: 1949.* Washington, D.C.: U.S. Government Printing Office, 1964, p. 485.

pp. 34–36: Dean Acheson, "Letter of Transmittal," *The China White Paper, August 1949.* Originally issued as *United States Relations with China, With Special Reference to the Period 1944–1949.* Dept. of State Publication 3573, Far Eastern Series 30. Stanford, Calif.: Stanford University Press, 1967, pp. iii–xvii.

pp. 36–38: "A Report to the President Pursuant to the President's Directive of January 31, 1950 [NSC-68], April 7, 1950," *Foreign Relations of the United States: 1950: Volume I: National Security Affairs, Foreign Economic Policy.* Washington, D.C.: U.S. Government Printing Office, 1977, pp. 235–92.

pp. 39–40: "Statement by the President on the Situation in Korea, June 27, 1950," *Public Papers of the Presidents of the United States: Harry S. Truman: 1950.* Washington, D.C.: U.S. Government Printing Office, 1965, p. 492.

pp. 40–41: Quoted in William Manchester, *American Caesar: Douglas MacArthur, 1880–1964.* New York: Dell, 1978, p. 764.

pp. 41–42: Quoted in Harry S Truman, *Memoirs: Volume Two: Years of Trial and Hope, 1946–1952.* Garden City, N.Y.: Doubleday, 1956, p. 449.

p. 42: Douglas MacArthur, *Reminiscences.* New York: McGraw-Hill, 1964, pp. 400–5.

p. 43: James A. Michener, *The Bridges at Toko-Ri.* New York: Random House, 1953, pp. 43–44.

pp. 46–49: House Committee on Un-American Activities, *Hearings Regarding the Communist Infiltration of the Motion Picture Industry*, 80th Cong., 1st Sess., October 27, 1947, 479–82.

pp. 49–50: "The Waldorf Statement," in Larry Ceplair and Steven Englund, *The Inquisition in Hollywood: Politics in the Film Community, 1930–1960.* Garden City, N.Y.: Doubleday, 1980, p. 445.

pp. 50–52: House Committee on Un-American Activities, *Hearings Regarding Communist Espionage in the United States Government*, 80th Cong., 2nd sess., August 3, 1948, 563–84.

pp. 52–56: House Committee on Un-American Activities, *Hearings Regarding Communist Espionage in the United States Government*, 80th Cong., 2nd sess., August 5, 1948, 642–59.

pp. 56–58: Judge Irving Kaufman, sentencing statement, April 5, 1951, in Transcript of Record, No. 111: "Julius Rosenberg and Ethel Rosenberg, Petitioners, vs. The United States of America" and No. 112: "Morton Sobell, Petitioner, vs. The United States of America," Supreme Court of the United States, October Term, 1951, Vol. 2, pp. 1612–1616. Reprint, 1952, National Committee to Secure Justice in the Rosenberg Case, in U.S. District Court, Southern District of New York, March 6–April 6, 1951.

pp. 58–60: Letters, Ethel Rosenberg to Julius Rosenberg, February 26, 1952, and Julius Rosenberg to Ethel Rosenberg, May 31, 1953. In Robert and Michael Meeropol, *We Are Your Sons: The Legacy of Ethel and Julius Rosenberg, written by their children Robert and Michael Meeropol.* Boston: Houghton Mifflin, 1975, pp. 128, 206–7. Used by permission of Robert and Michael Meeropol.

pp. 60–62: *Congressional Record.* 81st Cong., 2nd sess. 1951. Vol. 96, pt. 2, pp. 1954, 1956.

pp. 62–64: George H. Gallup, *The Gallup Poll: Public Opinion, 1935–1971. Vol. 2, 1949–1948.* New York: Random House, 1972, pp. 911–12, 1203. Copyright © 1972 by American Institute of Public Opinion. Reprinted by permission of Random House, Inc.

pp. 64–65: Arthur Miller, *The Crucible.* New York: Viking, 1952, pp. 5, 7, 141–43. Copyright © 1952, 1953, 1954, renewed © 1980, 1981, 1982 by Arthur Miller. Used by permission of Viking Penguin, a division of Penguin Putnam, Inc.

pp. 65–66: *High Noon.* 16mm, 85 min. Stanley Kramer for United Artists, 1952.

pp. 66–68: U.S. Senate, *Hearings Before the Special Subcommittee on Investigations of the Committee on Government Operations* [on Charges and Countercharges involving Secretary of the Army Robert T. Stevens, John G. Adams, H. Struve

Hensel, and Senator Joe McCarthy, Roy M. Cohn, and Francis P. Carr], 83rd Cong., 2nd sess., June 9, 1954, pp. 2427–2429.

pp. 68–69: *Congressional Record.* 83rd Cong., 2nd sess. 1954. Vol. 100, pt. 12, p. 16392.

pp. 72–73: "Inaugural Address, January 20, 1953," *Public Papers of the Presidents of the United States: Dwight D. Eisenhower: 1953.* U.S. Government Printing Office, 1960, pp. 1–4.

pp. 73–74: John Foster Dulles, "A Policy of Boldness," *Life*, May 19, 1952. Vol. 32: pp. 146, 149, 152, 154. © 1952 Time Inc. Reprinted by permission.

pp. 74–76: NSC 162/2, October 30, 1953, in *The Pentagon Papers: The Defense Department History of United States Decision making on Vietnam*, ed. Senator Gravel. Vol. 1. Boston: Beacon, 1971, pp. 416, 417, 426.

pp. 76–77: "President's News Conference of April 7, 1954," *Public Papers of the Presidents of the United States: Dwight D. Eisenhower: 1954.* Washington, D.C.: U.S. Government Printing Office, 1960, pp. 382–83.

pp. 79–80: Billy Graham, "Satan's Religion." *American Mercury:* 79 (August 1954): pp. 41, 42, 46.

pp. 81–82: Tom Lehrer, *Too Many Songs by Tom Lehrer* . New York: Pantheon, 1981, pp. 20–21, 86–87. Album 1, "Songs by Tom Lehrer," No. 6216, Reprise. Album 2, "An Evening Wasted with Tom Lehrer," No. 6199, Reprise. Courtesy of Tom Lehrer.

pp. 82–85: Dwight D. Eisenhower, "Farewell Radio and Television Address to the American People." January 17, 1961. *Public Papers of the Presidents of the United States: Dwight D. Eisenhower: 1960–1961.* Washington, D.C.: U.S. Government Printing Office, 1961, pp. 1036–1039.

pp. 85–87: "Inaugural Address. January 20, 1961." *Public Papers of the Presidents of the United States: John F. Kennedy: 1961.* Washington, D.C.: U.S. Government Printing Office, 1962, pp. 1–3.

pp. 87–88: "The President's News Conference of April 12, 1961." *Public Papers of the Presidents of the United States: John F. Kennedy: 1961.* Washington, D.C.: U.S. Government Printing Office, 1962, pp. 258–59.

pp. 88–89: "Address Before the American Society of Newspaper Editors, April 20, 1961. *Public Papers of the Presidents of the United States: John F. Kennedy: 1961.* Washington, D.C.: U.S. Government Printing Office, 1962, p. 304.

pp. 90–91: "Remarks in the Rudolph Wilde Platz, Berlin, June 26, 1963." *Public Papers of the Presidents of the United States: John F. Kennedy: 1963.* Washington, D.C.: U.S. Government Printing Office, 1964, pp. 524–25.

pp. 93–95: "Radio and Television Report to the American People on the Soviet Arms Buildup in Cuba, October 22, 1962." *Public Papers of the Presidents of the United States: John F. Kennedy: 1962.*

Washington, D.C.: U.S. Government Printing Office, 1963, pp. 806–9.

pp. 108–9: Ho Chi Minh, "Declaration of Independence of the Democratic Republic of Vietnam," September 2, 1945. In *Breaking Our Chains: Documents on the Vietnamese Revolution of August, 1945.* Hanoi, Vietnam: Foreign Language Publishing House, 1960, pp. 94–97. Reprinted in Steven Cohen, ed., *Anthology and Guide to a Television History.* New York: Knopf, 1983, pp. 24–26.

pp. 109–10: Franklin D. Roosevelt to Cordell Hull, January 24, 1944. In *The Pentagon Papers,* ed. Senator Gravel. Boston: Beacon Press, 1971, Vol. 1, p. 10.

pp. 110–11: Secretary of State to Embassy in France, February 3, 1947. In *Foreign Relations of the United States: 1947.* Vol. VI: *The Far East.* Washington, D.C.: U.S. Government Printing Office, 1972, pp. 67–68.

pp. 112–13: Dwight D. Eisenhower, *Mandate for Change, 1953–1956.* Garden City, N.Y.: Doubleday, 1963, p. 347.

pp. 113–15: "Final Declaration of the Geneva Conference," July 21, 1954. In *The Pentagon Papers,* ed. Senator Gravel. Boston: Beacon Press, 1971, Vol. 1, pp. 571–73.

pp. 115–16: President Eisenhower to President Diem, October 1, 1954. In Kahin, George McTurnan, and John W. Lewis, *The United States in Vietnam.* New York: Dial, 1967, pp. 382–83. Reprinted with permission.

pp. 116–17: John F. Kennedy, "America's Stake in Vietnam." Speech delivered June 1, 1956, at conference sponsored by American Friends of Vietnam. In *Vital Speeches of the Day,* 22 (August 1, 1956), p. 618. Reprinted with permission.

pp. 118–19: President Kennedy to President Diem, December 14, 1961. In *Department of State Bulletin 46* January 1, 1962, p. 13.

pp. 121–22: Lyndon B. Johnson, "Pattern for Peace in Southeast Asia," April 7, 1965. *Department of State Bulletin:* 52 (April 26, 1965), pp. 606–7.

pp. 122–23: Mark Baker, *Nam: The Vietnam War in the Words of the Men and Women Who Fought There.* New York: Quill, 1982, pp. 110–11. Reprinted with permission.

pp. 123–25: *New York Times,* November 25, 1969. Copyright © 1996 by the New York Times Co. Reprinted by permission.

pp. 126–28: "I-Feel-Like-I'm-Fixin'-to-Die Rag" by Joe McDonald. Copyright 1965, renewed 1993 by Alkatraz Corner Music/BMI. Words and music by Joe McDonald. Used by permission.

pp. 128–30: "Address to the Nation on the Situation in Southeast Asia," April 30, 1970. *Public Papers of the Presidents of the United States: Richard Nixon: 1970.* Washington, D.C.: U.S. Government Printing Office, 1971, pp. 405–10.

pp. 130–31: "Agreement on Ending the War and Restoring Peace in Vietnam," Paris, January 27, 1973. *Weekly Compilation of Presidential Documents.* Vol. 9: 4 (January 29, 1973): pp. 45–50.

pp. 133–36: "Treaty Banning Nuclear Weapon Tests in the Atmosphere, in Outer Space and Under Water." In Stanford Arms Control Group, *International Arms Control: Issues and Agreements.* 2nd ed., eds. Coit D. Blacker and Gloria Duffy. Stanford, Calif.: Stanford University Press, 1984, pp. 366–68.

pp. 136–39: "Treaty Between the United States of America and the Union of Soviet Socialist Republics on the Limitation of Anti-Ballistic Missile Systems, and Interim Agreement Between the United States of America and the Union of Soviet Socialist Republics on Certain Measures with Respect to the Limitation of Strategic Offensive Arms." In Stanford Arms Control Group, *International Arms Control: Issues and Agreements.* 2nd ed., eds. Coit D. Blacker and Gloria Duffy. Stanford, Calif.: Stanford University Press, 1984, pp. 413–20.

pp. 139–40: "Treaty Between the United States of America and the Union of Soviet Socialist Republics on the Limitation of Strategic Offensive Arms." In Stanford Arms Control Group, *International Arms Control: Issues and Agreements.,* 2nd ed., eds. Coit D. Blacker and Gloria Duffy. Stanford, Calif.: Stanford University Press, 1984, pp. 446–69.

pp. 140–42: "Remarks at the Annual Convention of the National Association of Evangelicals in Orlando, Florida," March 8, 1983. In *Public Papers of the Presidents of the United States: Ronald Reagan: 1983.* Book I. Washington, D.C.: U.S. Government Printing Office, 1984, pp. 363–64.

pp. 142–43: "Address to the Nation on Defense and National Security," March 23, 1983. In *Public Papers of the Presidents of the United States: Ronald Reagan: 1983.* Book 1. Washington, D.C.: U.S. Government Printing Office, 1984, pp. 442–43.

pp. 144–45: "Address Before a Joint Session of the Congress on the State of the Union," January 28, 1992. In *Public Papers of the Presidents of the United States: George Bush: 1992–1993.* Book I. Washington, D.C.: U.S. Government Printing Office, 1993, pp. 156–57.

Sidebars

p. 18: Albert Einstein quoted in Martin J. Sherwin, *A World Destroyed: The Atomic Bomb and the Grand Alliance.* New York: Knopf, 1975, p. 27.

p. 19: Harry S. Truman, *Memoirs: Volume One: Year of Decisions.* Garden City, N.Y.: Doubleday, 1955, p. 82.

p. 22: Henry A. Wallace quoted in Daniel Yergin, *Shattered Peace: The Origins of the Cold War and the National Security State.* Boston: Houghton Mifflin, 1977, p. 445, n. 41.

p. 24: George Kennan quoted in Melvyn P. Leffler, *A Preponderance of Power: National Security, the Truman Administration, and the Cold War.* Stanford, Calif.: Stanford University Press, 1992, p. 108.

p. 25: Walter Lippmann quoted in Walter LaFeber, *America, Russia, and the Cold War, 1945–1966.* New York: Wiley, 1967, p. 54.

p. 28 (top): Dean Acheson, *Present at the Creation: My Years in the State Department.* New York: Norton, 1969, p. 293.

p. 28 (bottom): Arthur Vandenberg quoted in Dean Acheson, *Present at the Creation: My Years in the State Department.* New York: Norton, 1969, p. 293.

p. 30: Averell Harriman quoted in Melvyn P. Leffler, *A Preponderance of Power: National Security, the Truman Administration, and the Cold War.* Stanford, Calif.: Stanford University Press, 1992, p. 162.

p. 31: Instructions reproduced Ralph B. Levering, Vladimir O. Pechatnov, Verena Botzenhart-Viehe, and C. Earl Edmondson, *Debating the Origins of the Cold War: American and Russian Perspectives.* New York: Rowman and Littlefield, 2002, p. 168.

p. 33 (top): Report reproduced in Ralph B. Levering, Vladimir O. Pechatnov, Verena Botzenhart-Viehe, and C. Earl Edmondson, *Debating the Origins of the Cold War: American and Russian Perspectives.* New York: Rowman and Littlefield, 2002, p 176.

p. 33 (bottom): Harold Urey quoted in Eric F. Goldman, *The Crucial Decade—and After: America, 1945–1960.* New York: Vintage, 1960, p. 100.

p. 34: Sergei N. Goncharov, John W. Lewis, and Xue Litai, *Uncertain Partners: Stalin, Mao, and the Korean War.* Stanford, Calif.: Stanford University Press, 1993, p. 3.

p. 35: *New York Times,* August 22, 1949.

p. 36: Kenneth Wherry quoted in Eric F. Goldman, *The Crucial Decade—and After: America, 1945–1960.* New York: Vintage, 1960, p. 116.

p. 38: Dean Acheson, *Present at the Creation: My Years in the State Department.* New York: Signet, 1970, p. 488.

p. 40: Harry S. Truman, *Memoirs: Volume Two: Years of Trial and Hope, 1946–1952.* Garden City, N.Y.: Doubleday, 1956, p. 332–33.

p. 41: Omar N. Bradley and Clay Blair, *A General's Life: An Autobiography.* New York: Simon & Schuster, 1983, p. 558.

p. 42: Robert Kerr quoted in William Manchester, *American Caesar: Douglas MacArthur, 1880–1964.* New York: Dell, 1978, p. 765.

p. 43: From *The Manchurian Candidate.* 126 min. United Artists, 1962.

p. 51: Hiss telegram quoted in Allen Weinstein, *Perjury: The Hiss–Chambers Case.* New York: Knopf, 1978, p. 8.

p. 52: Richard M. Nixon, *Six Crises.* Garden City, N.Y.: Doubleday, 1962, pp. 7–8.

p. 53: In Allen Weinstein, *Perjury: The Hiss–Chambers Case.* New York: Knopf, 1978, p. 15.

p. 54: Richard M. Nixon, *Six Crises*. Garden City, N.Y.: Doubleday, 1962, p. 62.

p. 56 (top): Cable quoted in John Earl Haynes and Harvey Klehr, *Venona: Decoding Soviet Espionage in America*. New Haven, Conn.: Yale University Press, 2000, pp. 309–10.

p. 56 (bottom): Ronald Radosh and Joyce Milton, *The Rosenberg Trial: A Search for the Truth*. New York: Holt, Rinehart & Winston, 1983, pp. 284–85.

p. 61: From Richard H. Rovere, *Senator Joe McCarthy*. New York: World, 1960, pp. 135–36.

p. 62: *Congressional Record*, 82nd Cong., 1st sess., 1951. Vol. 97, pt. 5, p. 6556.

p. 64: In Ronald Radosh and Joyce Milton, *The Rosenberg Trial: A Search for the Truth*. New York: Holt, Rinehart & Winston, 1983, p. 389.

p. 68: Margaret Chase Smith, *Declaration of Conscience*, ed. William C. Lewis, Jr. Garden City, N.Y.: Doubleday, 1972, pp. 12–18.

p. 72: Eisenhower quoted in Robert A. Divine, *Eisenhower and the Cold War*. New York: Oxford University Press, 1981, p. 15.

p. 73: Eisenhower quoted in Emmet John Hughes, *The Ordeal of Power: A Political Memoir of the Eisenhower Years*. New York: Atheneum, 1975, p. 251.

p. 74 (top): Nikita S. Khrushchev, *Khrushchev Remembers: The Glasnost Tapes*, edited and translated by Jerrold L. Schecter with Vyacheslav V. Luchkov. Boston: Little, Brown, 1990, pp. 100–1.

p. 74 (bottom): John Foster Dulles, "The Evolution of Foreign Policy." Address given before Council on Foreign Relations, New York, January 12, 1954. Department of State Bulletin 30 (January 25, 1954): p. 108.

p. 75: George Humphrey quoted in Douglas Kinnard, *President Eisenhower and Strategy Management: A Study in Defense Politics*. Lexington: University Press of Kentucky, 1977, p. 27.

p. 76: "Remarks at the 42d Annual Meeting of the United States Chamber of Commerce, April 26, 1954," *Public Papers of the Presidents of the United States: Dwight D. Eisenhower: 1954*. Washington, D.C.: U.S. Government Printing Office, 1960, pp. 421–22.

p. 77: In James T. Patterson, *Grand Expectations: The United States, 1945–1974*. New York: Oxford University Press, 1996, pp. 306–7.

p. 78 (top): Nikita S. Khrushchev, *Khrushchev Remembers*, edited and translated by Strobe Talbot. New York: Bantam, 1971, p. 472.

p. 78 (bottom): In James T. Patterson, *America Since 1941: A History*. New York: Harcourt Brace, 1994, p. 105.

p. 79: Billy Graham quoted in David Chidester, *Patterns of Power: Religion and Politics in American Culture*. Englewood Cliffs, N.J.: Prentice Hall, 1988, p. 276.

p. 81: Lewis Strauss quoted in Robert A. Divine, *Blowing on the Wind: The Nuclear Test Ban Debate, 1954–1960*. New York: Oxford University Press, 1978, pp. 11–12.

p. 84: Scott Russell Sanders, *Hunting for Hope: A Father's Journey*. Boston: Beacon Press, 1998.

p. 85: John F. Kennedy, "Special Message to the Congress on Urgent National Needs," May 25, 1961. *Public Papers of the Presidents of the United States: John F. Kennedy: 1961*. Washington, D.C.: U.S. Government Printing Office, 1962, p. 404.

p. 86: John F. Kennedy quoted in Richard J. Walton, *Cold War and Counterrevolution: The Foreign Policy of John F. Kennedy*. Baltimore: Penguin, 1973, p. 9.

p. 88: Quoted in Arthur M. Schlesinger, Jr., *A Thousand Days: John F. Kennedy in the White House*. Boston: Houghton Mifflin, 1965, p. 251.

p. 89 (top): C. Wright Mills quoted in Arthur M. Schlesinger, Jr., *A Thousand Days: John F. Kennedy in the White House*. Boston: Houghton Mifflin, 1965, p. 286.

p. 89 (bottom): Pierre Salinger quoted in James T. Patterson, *Grand Expectations: The United States, 1945–1974*. New York: Oxford University Press, 1996, p. 494.

p. 90: "Radio and Television Report to the American People on the Berlin Crisis, July 25, 1961." *Public Papers of the Presidents of the United States: John F. Kennedy: 1961*. Washington, D.C.: U.S. Government Printing Office, 1962, p. 534.

p. 92: Robert Kennedy quoted in Stephen E. Ambrose, *Rise to Globalism: American Foreign Policy Since 1938*, 3rd ed. New York: Penguin, 1983, pp. 262–63.

p. 94 (top): Anatoly Dobrynin, *In Confidence: Moscow's Ambassador to America's Six Cold War Presidents (1962–1986)*. New York: Times Books, 1995, p.73.

p. 94 (bottom): Dean Rusk quoted in Stewart Alsop and Charles Bartlett, "In Time of Crisis." *Saturday Evening Post*, 235 (December 8, 1962), p. 16.

p. 108: Memorandum from William J. Donovan to Secretary of State, August 22, 1945. In House Committee on Armed Services, *United States–Vietnam Relations, 1945–1967: Study Prepared by the Department of Defense*. Washington, D.C.: U.S. Government Printing Office, 1971, Book 8, pp. 45–47.

p. 109 (top): Giap quoted in R. Harris Smith, *OSS: The Secret History of America's First Central Intelligence Agency*. Berkeley: University of California Press, 1972, p. 354.

p. 109 (bottom): Nikita S. Khrushchev, *Khrushchev Remembers*, edited and translated by Strobe Talbot. New York: Bantam, 1971, p. 531.

p. 110 (top): Winston Churchill quoted in Robert M. Hathaway, *Ambiguous Partnership: Britain and America, 1944–1947*. New York: Columbia University Press, 1981, p. 45.

p. 110 (bottom): Office of Strategic Services, "Problems of United States Policy," April 2, 1945. In George C. Herring, *America's Longest War: The United States and Vietnam, 1950–1975*. New York: Wiley, 1979, p. 6.

p. 111: Department of State Policy Statement on Indochina, September 27, 1948. In *Foreign Relations of the United States: 1948*. Vol. VI: *The Far East and Australia*. Washington, D.C.: U.S. Government Printing Office, 1974, p. 48.

p. 112: A. C. Davis quoted in *The Pentagon Papers*, ed. Senator Gravel. Boston: Beacon Press, 1971, Vol. 1, p. 89.

p. 113 (top): John F. Kennedy quoted in Alexander Kendrick, *The Wound Within: America in the Vietnam Years, 1945–1974*. Boston: Little, Brown, 1974, p. 66.

p. 113 (bottom): Townsend Hoopes, *The Devil and John Foster Dulles: The Diplomacy of the Eisenhower Era*. Boston: Little, Brown, 1973, p. 222.

p. 114: John Foster Dulles quoted in George C. Herring, *America's Longest War: The United States and Vietnam, 1950–1975*. New York: Wiley, 1979, p. 38.

p. 115: Dwight Eisenhower quoted in George C. Herring, *America's Longest War: The United States and Vietnam, 1950–1975*. New York: Wiley, 1979, p. 42.

p. 117: Milton C. Taylor, "South Vietnam: Lavish Aid, Limited Progress." *Pacific Affairs*: 34 (Fall 1961), p. 256.

p. 118: Lyndon Johnson quoted in Arthur M. Schlesinger, Jr., *A Thousand Days: John F. Kennedy in the White House*. Boston: Houghton Mifflin, 1965, p. 542.

p. 121 (top): Lyndon B. Johnson quoted in Tom Wicker, *JFK and LBJ: The Influence of Personality upon Politics*. New York: Morrow, 1968, p. 205.

p. 121 (bottom): Bao Ninh, *The Sorrow of War: A Novel*. Frank Palmos, ed. From the original translation by Phan Thanh Hao. London: Vintage, 1993, p. 2.

p. 122: Lyndon B. Johnson quoted in Doris Kearns, *Lyndon Johnson and the American Dream*. New York: Harper & Row, 1976, pp. 251–52.

p. 122: Philip Caputo, *A Rumor of War*. New York: Holt, 1977, p. xviii.

p. 123: Ron Kovic, *Born on the Fourth of July*. New York: McGraw-Hill, 1976, p. 11.

p. 124: Quoted in Gary Nash et al., *The American People: Creating a Nation and a Society*, 4th ed. New York: Longman, 1998, p. 981.

p. 125: Philip Caputo, *A Rumor of War*. New York: Holt, 1977, p. 304.

p. 127: Lieutenant Dao An Tuat quoted in Jon Swain, *River of Time*. London, Minerva, 1966, p. 41.

p. 130: Quoted in Joseph Heller, *Good as Gold*. New York: Dell, 1985, p. 333.

p. 135: John F. Kennedy quoted in Herbert S. Parmet, *JFK: The Presidency of John F. Kennedy*. New York: Dial, 1983, p. 310.

p. 137: Richard M. Nixon, *RN: The Memoirs of Richard Nixon*. Vol. 2. New York: Warner, 1978, p. 91.

p. 139: "Address before the General Assembly," October 4, 1977. In *Public Papers of the Presidents of the United States: Jimmy Carter: 1971*, Book 2. Washington, D.C.: U.S. Government Printing Office, 1978, p.

p. 139: "Address before the General Assembly," October 4, 1977. In *Public Papers of the Presidents of the United States: Jimmy Carter: 1971*, Book 2. Washington, D.C.: U.S. Government Printing Office, 1978, p. 1716.

p. 140: Quoted in Allan M. Winkler, *Life Under a Cloud: American Anxiety about the Atom*. New York: Oxford University Press, 1993, p. 189.

p. 142: Russell Baker, "Nuclear Experts Need Dose of Doubt," *Eugene* [Ore.] *Register-Guard*, December 13, 1982.

p. 143: William Safire, "New Name for 'Star Wars,'" *New York Times Magazine*, March 24, 1985, p. 14.

p. 144: William H. Webster quoted in Walter LaFeber, *America, Russia, and the Cold War, 1945–1996*, 8th ed. New York: McGraw-Hill, 1997, p. 335.

p. 145: "Excerpts from News Conference," Camp David, Md., February 1, 1992. In *U.S. Department of State Dispatch* 3 (February 3, 1992), p. 78.

Picture Credits

AP/Wide World Photos: 119, 126, 127; Archive Photos: 83; From *Red Scared!*/The Michael Barson Collection: 48, 49; Bettmann/Corbis: 47, 57, 58, 59; Bundesarchiv, Koblenz: 31; George Bush Presidential Library: 9, 132, 145; Courtesy, Jimmy Carter Library: 139; Reproduced from a copy in the Churchill Papers, Churchill Archives Centre, Cambridge: 12; Corbis/Bettmann-UPI: 63, 87, 129; Dallas Notes: 130; Department of Defense: 142, 147; © Disney Enterprises, Inc.: 104; Florida State Archives: 15; Hake's Americana & Collectibles: 21, 92, 146; John F. Kennedy Library: 86 (SC 578833), 90 (DX65-105-132), 95, 147 (DX65-105-132); LBJ Library Collection: 120 (photo by Yoichi R. Okamoto), 128 (photo by Jack Kightlinger); Courtesy of Tom Lehrer, cover design by Eric Martin: 82; Library of Congress, Prints and Photographs Division: 19 (USZ62-101609), 20 (USZ62-119708), 26 (USZ62-117301), 29, 32, 33, 35, 37, 44 (USZ62-113251), 53, 54, 64, 69, 72 (USZ62-090397), 75, 78, 79, 80, 88 (USZ62-101477), 93, 108, 112, 114, 115, 116, 117, 118, 125, 134, 135; © Edwin Marcus: 9, 34; Marshall and Scott Drawings: 104; © 2000 Marvel Characters, Inc. All rights reserved: 101; Maytag Corporation: 14; Walter Havinghurst Special Collections, Miami University Library: 50; MOMA Film Stills: 100, 146; National Archives Still Picture Branch: 3, 39, 40, 96, 98, 99, 103, 105, 106, 111, 123, 137, 138; National Park Service: 131; New York Times: 2; The Richard Nixon Library and Birthplace Foundation: 136; Photofest: 43, 65, 140; Princeton University Library, University Archives, Department of Rare Books and Special Collections: 5, 124; Private Collection: 70; Courtesy Ronald Reagan Library: 143; Reuters/David Brauchli/Archive Photos: 144; Franklin D. Roosevelt Library: 18, 19; Peter Stackpole/LIFE/TimePix: 100; The Swarthmore Peace Collection: 102, 141; Gary Tong: 41;

© Tribune Media Services, Inc. All Rights Reserved. Reprinted with permission: 91; Courtesy, Harry S. Truman Library: 10 (National Park Service photograph by Abbie Rowe), 16 (U.S. Army photograph), 21 (photograph by Terry Savage), 23, 102; The University College London, School of Slavonic and East European Studies: 36; © 1947 *The Washington Post*. Reprinted with permission: 30; Herblock, © 1955 The Washington Post Co., from *Herblock's Here and Now* (Simon & Schuster, 1955): 102; Herblock, © 1956 The Washington Post Co., from *Herblock's Special For Today* (Simon & Schuster, 1958): 77; Herblock, © 1959 The Washington Post Co., from *Herblock: A Cartoonist's Life* (Times Books, 1998): 67.

Although every effort has been made to secure permission for text and picture usage, we may have failed in a few cases to trace the copyright holder. We apologize for any apparent negligence

Index

Acknowledgments

This book had its origin in a conversation with Nancy Toff at an Oxford University Press party at the American Historical Association convention in New York several years ago. Since that time, Nancy has been helpful at every juncture, with ideas and suggestions that have improved the manuscript. I would like to thank as well series editor Sarah Deutsch for her recommendations over the past several years, and Lisa Barnett of Oxford University Press for helping move the book through production.

I am also grateful to Sara, my wife, for her good humor and assistance in helping me keep a sense of perspective when I get bogged down, and to my sister Karen, to whom this book is dedicated, for her editorial assistance on all kinds of projects over the years.

About the Author

Allan M. Winkler is Distinguished Professor of History at Miami University in Ohio. He has also taught at Yale University and the University of Oregon and, for one year each, at the University of Helsinki in Finland, the University of Amsterdam in The Netherlands, and the University of Nairobi in Kenya. A prize-winning teacher, he is author of seven books of his own, which include *The Politics of Propaganda: The Office of War Information, 1942-1945; Home Front U.S.A.: America during World War II;* and *Life Under a Cloud: American Anxiety about the Atom,* and co-author of the college textbook *The American People: Creating a Nation and a Society* and the high school textbook *America: Pathways to the Present.*